CONTENTS

T0004096

DIP DIP HOORAY!............ **22**

THE ULTIMATE
TAILGATING
PLAYBOOK

THE UL

TAILG

PLAY

TIMATE
ATING
BOOK

(75) RECIPES THAT WIN EVERY TIME

RUSS T. FENDER

UNION
SQUARE
& CO.

NEW YORK

UNION
SQUARE
& CO.

NEW YORK

UNION SQUARE & CO. and the distinctive Union Square & Co. logo are
trademarks of Sterling Publishing Co., Inc.

Union Square & Co., LLC, is a subsidiary of Sterling Publishing Co., Inc.

ISBN 978-1-4549-4642-7
ISBN 978-1-4549-4644-1 (e-book)

Library of Congress Cataloging-in-Publication Data

Title: The ultimate tailgating playbook : 75 recipes that win every time.
Description: New York, NY : Union Square & Co., [2022] | Includes index. |
    Summary: "A handy guide that's everything needed to turn a tailgate
    party into a great one. Included are important lessons like packing a
    cooler and manning the grill, as well as 75 delicious recipes.
    Throughout are hints, tricks, and tips for making every dish a success.
    There are recipes for dips, apps, soups, salads, rib-sticking mains,
    desserts ranging from no-bake to show-off, and a variety of mixed drinks
    including beer cocktails, Bloody Marys, and plenty of rounds of shots in
    between. The food is all over the map, literally, from the South (Down
    South Pimento Cheese), to the North (New England Clam Chowder), the
    Midwest (Wisconsin Booyah), the Southwest (Southwest Chili Verde), and
    Cali vibes (Guaca de Gallo)"-- Provided by publisher.
Identifiers: LCCN 2022001148 (print) | LCCN 2022001149 (ebook) | ISBN
    9781454946427 (paperback) | ISBN 9781454946441 (epub)
Subjects: LCSH: Tailgate parties. | LCGFT: Cookbooks.
Classification: LCC TX823 .U48 2022 (print) | LCC TX823 (ebook) | DDC
    642/.3--dc23/eng/20220213
LC record available at https://lccn.loc.gov/2022001148
LC ebook record available at https://lccn.loc.gov/2022001149

For information about custom editions, special sales, and premium purchases,
please contact specialsales@unionsquareandco.com.

Manufactured in Canada

2 4 6 8 10 9 7 5 3 1

unionsquareandco.com

Image credits: pgs. 20–21, 170–171, 174–175, 178–179,
180–181, 184–185: Oxy_gen/Shutterstock.com

Cover and interior design by Raphael Geroni

THE MAIN EVENT

SIDELINES

INTRODUCTION

CLEAR EYES, FULL BELLIES, CAN'T LOSE.

THAT'S OUR MOTTO, AND WE'RE STICKING TO it. Welcome to your handy guide for everything you've ever needed to turn a tailgate into a tail*great*. (Trigger warning: Dad jokes ahead.) We'll guide you through all the equipment you need to score big. We'll huddle up for important lessons like packing a cooler and manning the grill. We'll hand over the playbook for the recipes that are guaranteed to make you the MVP of every outing. And we'll even coach from the sidelines with hints, tricks, and tips to make every dish a touchdown.

Before we get into all that, a quick history: college football dates back to a Rutgers vs. Princeton game played in New Jersey in 1869. (Rutgers won 6–4.) Even in those pre-historic times, the concept of gathering for a game included a party atmosphere with food and refreshments on the sidelines. But it wasn't until the mid-1900s, when cars became a common item—and more specifically, the spacious station wagons of the 1940s and '50s—that the parking-lot pregame with drinks and snacks became a true part of the tradition. And then, blah blah blah boring boring boring, we arrive at the 1980s and '90s, when tailgating really popped off. Grills became portable, coolers grew wheels, and the tailgate turf wars began. Now, tents, decorations, and a little friendly showboating are as common as grill smoke and the harmonious crack-open sound of a beer can. These days, with our abundance of technology and gadgetry, weekend warriors can practically move half of their house to the stadium lot. (There's a reason why, on average, 30 percent of tailgaters never make it to the stadium.)

But for now, you can forget about the generators and satellite TVs and dive into the depths of this book. You'll find dips, apps, soups (it gets cold out there!), salads, rib-sticking mains (including the easiest actual ribs you've ever made on page 107), desserts ranging from no-bake to show-off, and a variety of mixed drinks including beer cocktails, Bloody Marys, and *plenty* of rounds of shots in between. (Hey—don't read that chapter if you're under twenty-one!)

There are plenty of things to make ahead and bring to the game, like a French Onion Dip (page 25) that's so much better than the jarred stuff or Overtime Snack Mix (page 52) that will have everyone still snacking way past overtime. There are showstoppers to throw on the grill, like Spicy Beer Can Chicken (page 114) or Blistered Shishito Peppers (page 137). There are even things for the true fanatics, like Spirit Deviled Eggs (page 46) and Gridiron Cake (page 165).

The food here is all over the map—literally. We've got the South (Down South Pimento Cheese, page 29), the Northeast (New England Clam Chowder, page 98), the Midwest (Wisconsin Booyah, page 101), the Southwest (Southwest Chili Verde, page 90), and Cali vibes, too (Guaca de Gallo, page 30). We have the dishes you know and love, like Walking Tacos (page 56), Classic Barbecue Chicken (page 117), and Cornbread Salad (page 130). And then some true surprises, the twists of all twists, the final quarter comebacks, like Mississippi Mud Cheesecake (page 156), Bloomin' Garlic Bread (page 45), Sloppy Joe Sub (page 116), and a Loaded Hot Dog Bar (page 108) beyond your wildest imagination.

But hey, all joking aside, tailgating is not about who wins or loses. It's about piling up your plate with good eats, spending quality time, and making memories that last. Just remember the principles of a successful tailgate: friends, food, and fun. With these three, you'll never miss.

ESSENTIAL GEAR

Star players know that the right equipment can make it or break it when they hit the lot. Here are our favorite tools for a successful tailgate.

1. **BIG COOLERS.** We take a deep-dive on the cooler (and why you need two) on page 15, but just trust us and GO BIG. It'll be worth it. Some even have dividers for cutting boards, cooking gear, and spices.

2. **A GRILL.** Gas, electric, coal, small, medium, large. Take your pick. It's not a must, but it is a pretty central part of tailgating. We cover everything you need to know about nailing it on the grill on page 16.

3. **CHIMNEY STARTER.** No shame in the lighter fluid game, but think of it this way: you can buy a chimney once, or you can buy fluid forever.

4. **GRILL BRUSH.** A clean grill is a happy grill. Don't even think about firing up until you have a brush on hand.

5. **FIRE EXTINGUISHER.** Safety first. Keep a small one in your trunk for any accidents.

6. **THERMOMETER.** Infrared thermometers (the ones with laser beams) are great for checking surface temperature, like your grill or skillet, or for getting oil to the ideal fry temp. But if you're looking to perfect your steak game or check on your chicken thighs, you'll want a more traditional meat thermometer that you can insert. There are some great Bluetooth options out there, too.

7. **CAST-IRON SKILLET.** A large cast-iron skillet is key for cooking on the grill without anything slipping through the cracks. Nonstick skillets won't be able to handle the intense heat, and stainless steel can be tricky. A good cast iron will sear to perfection every time—and last you forever.

8. **SPATULA and TONGS.** Find a good medium-length pair. If you go too long, food will be hard to control; too short and your arm hair may be in danger.

9. **PORTABLE SLOW COOKER.** This is the clutch play for keeping soups or drinks perfectly warm when the day is bitingly cold.

10. **PLASTIC CUPS.** Obviously! In addition to the classic, you may want shot glasses and rocks glasses as well.

11. **GLOVES.** When you're handling food and there's no sink nearby, disposable vinyl gloves are the MVPs. Heat-resistant grill gloves will prevent a fumble when you're matched with a hot grill and scorching skillets.

12. **CAMP TABLE.** Find an inexpensive, super-compact foldable table. When you have dips, apps, drinks, and burgers to lay out, you'll be grateful for the extra yard.

13. **BLUETOOTH SPEAKER.** You already know, but just a reminder.

TOUCHDOWN TIPS

Throughout this book you'll see a bunch of Touchdown Tips to help you up your game to the pro level. But the party can't start without a solid plan, so we're sharing some key advice at kickoff.

Plenty of recipes here can be made ahead, served at room temp, or assembled on the fly—and we're always going to encourage you to work smarter, not harder. But for a classic doing-it-right tailgate, two things are more important than everything else: the cooler and the grill. If either of those fail . . . well, let's just make sure that doesn't happen.

PACKING THE COOLER

A properly packed cooler is hyper important when hitting the great outdoors, because food poisoning is the ultimate party foul. (Warm drinks are pretty bad, too.) Here's a quick guide to your mobile refrigerator:

1. **DOUBLE UP.** Use one cooler for food and another for drinks. Let's be honest, everyone is going to be in and out of the drinks cooler all day, and after a few rounds that lid is probably staying open. If it's in its own cooler, the food can stay nice and cold without disturbance.

2. **GO BIG.** Invest in a large cooler that can fit a lot of food while still leaving a ton of room for ice. You want a 2:1 ice-to-food ratio. In other words, packing it all in and sprinkling a little ice over top isn't going to work.

3. **COOL IT DOWN.** This is a true pro move. The night before game day, fill your cooler with ice and seal it tight. Leave it in a cool place like a basement or even outside if it's cold enough at night. Dump out the ice before packing up; you'll be starting from cool.

4. **COLD FOOD ONLY.** Make sure everything that needs to be kept cold starts cold. Adding hot or warm food will increase the temp of the whole cooler and make it a playground for bacteria. Only items that were already refrigerated should go in.

5. **WORK IN LAYERS.** Line the bottom of the cooler with ice packs. Raw meat or extra-cold items go in next. Salads, dips, and sauces go in the middle surrounded by loose ice. Cheese, veggies, and condiments can go up top.

Finish with more ice packs or ice. (Conveniently, this is likely the order you'll be unpacking anyway.)

6. **LEAVE NO ROOM.** Empty space will encourage the ice to melt, so pack it in tight. Just be sure there's still room for the lid to shut tight because . . .

7. **CLOSE IT UP.** Keep that lid on and only go in when you need to. (Which is why we'll say it again for the people in the back: Get a separate cooler for drinks!)

◦ MANNING THE GRILL ◦

Being in charge of the grill is arguably as stressful as being a starting quarterback in the playoffs. The pressure is on, but every grill master will tell you that temperature control is the make-it-or-break-it of a successful barbecue. Here is an easy guide to nail it every time.

Lighting Charcoal

Whether you're using a chimney or lighter fluid, the key to lighting charcoal is letting it heat up thoroughly. Dark gray or black coals aren't ready; wait until they're glowing red and ashy white before you start cooking. If you're unsure, hold your hand about 5 inches above the coals. If you have to pull it back within 3 seconds, you're ready to go.

When using a chimney, fill the top with charcoal and stuff the base with newspaper, paper towels, napkins, or anything else easily flammable. Set the chimney on the grill grates and light the paper. The paper will ignite the bottom coals, and the heat will slowly rise up until all the coals are white-hot.

When using lighter fluid, pile the coals in the bottom of the grill, making a tight pyramid. Lightly coat the top layer of charcoal in lighter fluid, then let the coals sit for 5 minutes so the fluid drips down. Use a long match or lighter to light the coals from the bottom of the pyramid. Cover the grill, leaving the top and bottom vents fully open, until the coals are white-hot.

Oiling the Grates

Oil drips cause flare-ups, so easy does it. You want to lightly coat the grates so food doesn't stick—the key word being *lightly*. Wad up some paper towels and dip them in vegetable oil to coat, but do not saturate them to the point of a drippy mess. Pinch the oiled towels with tongs and wipe along the grates.

A GUIDE TO GRILL TEMPS

CHARCOAL

HIGH HEAT. Spread the hot coals across the entire bottom of the grill, leaving the top and bottom vents fully open. Let the grill fully heat with the lid down for at least 10 minutes, aiming for about 500°F, then rub the grates with oil.

MEDIUM HEAT. Spread the hot coals across the entire bottom of the grill, leaving the top vent fully open and the bottom vent half open. Let the grill fully heat with the lid down for at least 10 minutes, aiming for about 350°F, then rub the grates with oil.

HIGH DIRECT HEAT and INDIRECT HEAT. Pile the hot coals on only one half of the bottom of the grill, leaving the top and bottom vents fully open. Let the grill fully heat with the lid down for at least 10 minutes, aiming for about 500°F, then rub the grates with oil. The coals are your direct heat, the half without is the indirect safe zone.

MEDIUM DIRECT HEAT and INDIRECT HEAT. Pile the hot coals on only one half of the bottom of the grill, leaving the top vent fully open and bottom vent half open. Let the grill fully heat with the lid down for at least 10 minutes, aiming for about 350°F, then rub the grates with oil. The coals are your direct heat, the half without is the indirect safe zone.

GAS

HIGH HEAT. Turn all the burners to high and let the grill fully heat with the lid down for at least 10 minutes, aiming for about 500°F, then rub the grates with oil.

MEDIUM HEAT. Turn all the burners to medium and let the grill fully heat with the lid down for at least 10 minutes, aiming for about 350°F, then rub the grates with oil.

HIGH DIRECT HEAT and INDIRECT HEAT. Turn the burners on one side of the grill on high and leave the burners on the other side off. Let the grill fully heat with the lid down for at least 10 minutes, aiming for about 500°F, then rub the grates with oil. The flame is your direct heat, the half without is the indirect safe zone.

MEDIUM DIRECT HEAT and INDIRECT HEAT. Turn the burners on one side of the grill to medium and leave the burners on the other side off. Let the grill fully heat with the lid down for at least 10 minutes, aiming for about 350°F, then rub the grates with oil. The flame is your direct heat, the half without is the indirect safe zone.

Using a Grill as an Oven

To create an oven effect, set the grill for both direct and indirect heat. Use high for oven temps around 450°F and medium for oven temps around 350°F. Place the baking dish, skillet, or rimmed baking sheet on the indirect side of the grill for slow and even baking. Use cookware that's made for high-heat cooking, like cast-iron, steel, or aluminum.

To gently reheat a dish, place it on the top rack with the lid down. This can be done while cooking other items on the grates below.

Food should be over the flames or hot coals only for super high-intensity cooking.

Using a Grill as a Stove

To create a stove top, prepare the grill for high heat on one side and medium heat on the other. This is slightly easier with a gas grill, since temperature changes can be controlled as needed. If you're using a charcoal grill, spread most of the coals on the high-heat side and less than half the coals on the medium-heat side.

When it's time to cook, remove the lid and place the skillet or saucepan directly over the flames or coals. Be careful when cooking with oil or anything highly flammable, which can cause serious flare-ups. Deep-frying can be done directly on the grill, but make sure the pot is less than half full of oil, and use extreme caution when adding and removing food from the oil. One wrong splash could send the whole pot up in flames.

Cleaning the Grill

Cleanup is the worst part of any party, but it's the most important part of grilling. A clean grill will distribute heat evenly, cook food perfectly, and prevent any flare-ups next time. Here are a couple easy steps:

1. **BRUSH THE GRATES IMMEDIATELY.** Use a grill brush as soon as you're done cooking while the grill is still hot. The heat will help any remnants flake off easily.

2. **DISCARD THE ASH.** After the grill has cooled completely, empty out any remaining coals and ash. You want to start fresh every time.

3. **WASH THE GRATES.** This step is on an as-needed basis, but it's a good idea to do occasionally. Soak the grates in soap and hot water, then scrub thoroughly to remove any stuck-on grime.

4. **GET IN THERE.** Give the interior—from base to lid—a once-over with steel wool to get rid of any stuck-on grime. Hot soapy water can be used to scrub off any greasy buildup.

5. **DON'T FORGET THE OUTSIDE.** Use a sponge and hot soapy water to scrub the outside of the grill every time. It'll make sure any flare-ups stay on the inside (and keep your grill looking pretty).

6. **COVER IT UP.** Always use a grill cover to prevent rust and decay.

PLAYBOOKS

We worked out the perfect plan for every situation, so you're not making game-day calls. These menus make up some of our favorite formations. We recommend assigning everyone on your team one dish to make, because after all, teamwork makes the dream work.

All in Advance

Down South Pimento Cheese 29 | Overtime Snack Mix 52
BLT Biscuits 68 | Chicken Tortilla Soup 95
No Stress Make-Ahead Ribs 107 | Tricolor Pasta Salad 134
No-Bake Eclair Cake 159 | The Perfect Bloody 176

Grill Hard or Go Home

Buffalo Chicken Dip 37 | Grilled Jalapeño Poppers 59
Spicy Honey Wings 73 | Southwest Chile Verde 90
Classic Barbecue Chicken 117 | Blistered Shishito Peppers 137
Cowboy Cookies 160 | Ginger Shandy 173

Out in the Cold

Warm Red Pepper Jelly & Bacon Dip 41
Bloomin' Garlic Bread 45 | Mini Meatball Subs 66
New England Clam Chowder 98 | Sloppy Joe Sub 116
Root Beer Baked Beans 136 | Spiced Apple Bars 155
Hottie Toddy 182

Endless Summer

Guaca de Gallo 30 | Antipasti Skewers 53

Lemon Pepper Popcorn Chicken 80 | Cajun Gumbo 94

Spicy Beer Can Chicken 114 | Refreshing Watermelon Salad 133

S'mores Brownies 151 | Beergaritas 173

The Ultimate Classic

French Onion Dip 25 | Walking Tacos 56

Juicy Lucy Sliders 70 | Texas Chili con Carne 93

Loaded Hot Dog Bar 108 | Chopped Chicken Caesar Salad 145

Mississippi Mud Cheesecake 156 | Marychelada 176

Smells Like Team Spirit

Football Bean Dip 32 | Spirit Deviled Eggs 46

Soft Pretzel Bites with Beer Cheese 82

Wisconsin Booyah 101 | Cola Burgers 122

Cornbread Salad 130 | Team Colors Cake 149

Buffalo Mary 176

FRENCH ONION DIP

The dip to end all dips. The ultimate. The GOAT. French onion dip is a must for any and every social gathering. Sure, you could buy it in a jar, but this homemade version takes barely any effort. Sweet and savory caramelized onions mixed up in a tangy, creamy dip and topped with fried shallots? This is not a drill!

SERVES 8

4 tablespoons **extra-virgin olive oil**

4 large **yellow** or **Vidalia onions**, diced

2 tablespoons **soy sauce**

1 **shallot**, halved and thinly sliced

½ teaspoon **kosher salt**

1 (16-ounce) container **sour cream**

¼ cup **mayonnaise**

1 tablespoon **fresh lemon juice**

½ teaspoon **freshly ground black pepper**

1 tablespoon chopped **fresh chives**

Ridged potato chips, for serving

1. Heat 2 tablespoons of the oil in a large skillet over medium heat. When the oil shimmers, add the onions. Cook, stirring occasionally, until the onions are soft and starting to caramelize, 25 to 30 minutes. Add the soy sauce and continue cooking until the onions are very soft and jammy, about 10 minutes more. Remove the skillet from the heat.

2. While the onions cook, in a small skillet, combine the remaining 2 tablespoons oil and the shallots. Place the skillet over medium heat to warm the oil and shallots gradually. Cook, stirring occasionally, until the shallots are sizzling and starting to brown, about 10 minutes. Remove the skillet from the heat and season with ¼ teaspoon of the salt. Set aside to cool.

3. While the caramelized onions are still warm, whisk in the sour cream, mayonnaise, lemon juice, pepper, and the remaining ¼ teaspoon salt. Transfer the dip to a serving bowl. Spoon the frizzled shallots and their oil over top and sprinkle with the chives.

4. Cover the bowl tightly with plastic wrap and chill in the refrigerator for at least 1 hour and up to overnight. Serve with potato chips.

TOUCHDOWN TIP: *This dip gets better the longer it sits. Make it the night before for insane flavor on game day.*

CHILE-MANGO SALSA

Sweet, spicy, savory, salty . . . this salsa does everything delicious in one bowl. And with a mix of fresh and canned ingredients (including canned mango, the time-saver of the century), it takes almost no time to whip up. Sure, some people may look at you funny and tell you fruit doesn't belong in salsa. But to those people we say, More for us!

SERVES 8

1 small **red onion**, diced

2 tablespoons **fresh lime juice**

1 **jalapeño**, diced (and seeded, if desired)

1 (15-ounce) can **black beans**, drained and rinsed

1 (15.25-ounce) can **sweet corn**, drained and rinsed

1 (15-ounce) can **diced mango**, drained

¼ cup chopped **fresh cilantro**

1 teaspoon **ground cumin**

½ teaspoon **kosher salt**

Crumbled **cotija cheese**

Tortilla chips, for serving

1. In a medium bowl, combine the onion and lime juice and toss to coat. Let sit for about 10 minutes, until the onion has mellowed and lost its bite. Add the jalapeño, black beans, corn, mango, cilantro, cumin, and salt. Toss to combine well.

2. Top with cotija cheese and serve with tortilla chips.

PIMENTO CHEESE

Pimento cheese is as Southern as sweet tea. Also known as the pâté of the South, Carolina caviar, or a million other euphemisms, truthfully, this dish is not a fancy one. What it is, though, is some kind of alchemy, where a mismatched team of ingredients gets thrown together and become the stars of the season. And don't you dare let us catch you serving this with anything other than a sleeve of saltines! It's a hall of fame combo for a reason.

===== SERVES 8 =====

1 (4-ounce) jar **pimientos**, drained and finely chopped

1 (8-ounce) bag **shredded cheddar cheese**

½ cup **mayonnaise**

¼ cup **cream cheese**, room temperature

1 teaspoon **hot sauce** (we like Tabasco)

1 teaspoon **onion powder**

Saltine crackers, for serving

1. In a medium bowl, stir together the pimientos, cheddar cheese, mayonnaise, cream cheese, hot sauce, and onion powder until well combined.

2. Cover the bowl tightly with plastic wrap and chill in the refrigerator for at least 1 hour and up to overnight. Serve with saltines.

GUACA DE GALLO

For anyone who has ever tried to dip the same tortilla chip in the pico *and* the guac, we see you. We understand you. And this one goes out to you. This little bowl is a zippy pico de gallo, but avocado gets traded in at the last minute and plays like it's always been on the team. It's so delicious you'll start to question why it wasn't this way all along.

SERVES 8

1 (14.5-ounce) can **diced tomatoes**, drained

1 large **red onion**, diced

2 **jalapeños**, diced (and seeded, if desired)

½ cup chopped **fresh cilantro**

2 tablespoons **lime juice**

½ teaspoon **kosher salt**

2 **avocados**, diced

Tortilla chips, for serving

1. In a medium bowl, toss together the tomatoes, onion, jalapeños, cilantro, lime juice, and salt. Gently fold in the avocado, being careful not to mash the pieces.

2. Serve with tortilla chips.

TOUCHDOWN TIP: *If your avocados aren't quite ripe, place them in a paper bag with an apple. Roll the bag closed and store at room temperature for 12 hours for a guac-ready avocado!*

FOOTBALL BEAN DIP

This dip is the overachiever. Sure, the layers are easy to throw together (including a guacamole that's delicious enough to stand alone for the normal achievers out there), but as soon as the green field is down, it's crunch time. A football made of refried beans and sour cream is the break-the-internet dip of the season. It's almost too pretty to eat, but every tortilla chip will be screaming, "Put me in, coach!"

SERVES 8

1 (15.5-ounce) jar **chunky salsa**

1 (24-ounce) container **sour cream**

1 (1-ounce) package **taco seasoning**

1 (8-ounce) bag **shredded cheddar jack cheese**

3 cups **guacamole**, store-bought or homemade *(recipe follows)*

2 (16-ounce) cans **refried beans**

½ cup **sour cream**

Tortilla chips, for serving

1. In a medium bowl, whisk together the salsa, sour cream, and taco seasoning until fully combined. Transfer the salsa mixture to a large serving dish. Sprinkle the cheese on top to cover it completely. Spoon the guacamole over the cheese and smooth it into an even layer. Spoon the refried beans into the shape of a football on top of the guacamole.

2. Scrape the sour cream into a resealable zip-top bag. Snip a ½-inch corner off the bag and squeeze the sour cream over the "football" to create the laces and stripes.

3. Cover with plastic wrap and chill in the refrigerator for 1 hour. Serve with tortilla chips.

Guacamole

MAKES 3 CUPS

¼ medium **white onion**, finely chopped

1 **jalapeño**, seeded and finely chopped

1 **garlic clove**, finely chopped

¼ cup **fresh cilantro leaves**, finely chopped

Juice of 1 **lime**, plus more as needed

4 large ripe **avocados**

1 teaspoon **kosher salt**, plus more as needed

In a medium bowl, stir together the onion, jalapeño, garlic, cilantro, and lime juice. Add the avocado and use a fork to mash everything together.

Stir in the salt and taste for seasoning, adding more lime juice or salt as needed. Serve immediately.

TOUCHDOWN TIP: *This one is for the perfectionists out there. Trace the football shape in the guac first (you can always "erase" it). Then scoop the refried beans into a zip-top bag, snip off the corner, and follow the outline as you squeeze.*

CHEDDAR BACON RANCH DIP

Cheddar. Bacon. Ranch. Let that wash over you. Have you ever heard a more beautiful trio of words? There are no tricks here, nothing fancy, just a purely addictive dip and a guaranteed touchdown.

SERVES 8

8 strips **thick-cut bacon**, cooked

1 (8-ounce) bag **shredded cheddar cheese**

1 (8-ounce) package **cream cheese**, room temperature

1 cup **sour cream**

1 (1-ounce) packet **ranch seasoning**

2 **scallions**, thinly sliced

Kettle-style potato chips, for serving

1. In a food processor, combine the bacon, cheddar cheese, cream cheese, sour cream, and ranch seasoning. Pulse about six times, scraping down the sides as needed, to form a cohesive dip with some texture.

2. Transfer the dip to a serving bowl and fold in most of the scallions, holding back just a sprinkle. Garnish the dip with the reserved scallions.

3. Cover the bowl tightly with plastic wrap and chill in the refrigerator for at least 1 hour and up to overnight. Serve with kettle chips.

QUESO OVERLOAD

Doesn't it feel like the action of dipping was made just for queso? Nothing is better than a tortilla chip perfectly coated with the creamy, cheesy, and slightly spicy dip. Make it ahead and store in a foil pie dish so you can quickly reheat it on the grill and have a warm bowl of queso waiting to welcome everyone to the best tailgate of their lives.

SERVES 8

2 strips **thick-cut bacon**, diced

1 small **yellow onion**, diced

2 **garlic cloves**, minced

2 cups **whole milk**

8 ounces **cheddar cheese**, shredded

8 ounces **pepper jack cheese**, shredded

1 to 2 tablespoons **Mexican hot sauce**

¼ teaspoon **kosher salt**

Tortilla chips, for serving

1. Place the bacon in a medium saucepan. Set the pan over medium heat and cook the bacon, stirring occasionally, until the fat begins to render, about 1 minute. Add the onion and garlic and continue cooking until the bacon is crisp and the onions are starting to soften, about 3 minutes more.

2. Add the milk to the saucepan and bring to a simmer. Stir in both cheeses, the hot sauce, and the salt until the cheese is melted and the mixture is smooth.

3. Transfer to a serving bowl. Serve with tortilla chips.

TOUCHDOWN TIP: *Bags of pre-shredded cheese are coated in powders to prevent sticking. Buy a block of cheese and shred it yourself for a perfectly smooth finish.*

BUFFALO CHICKEN DIP

We've got the chicken, carrot, celery, blue cheese, and hot sauce here, but it's all mixed up in a creamy dip and blanketed in cheese for perfectly gooey ribbons every time you go in for a scoop. We're not going to say it's better than traditional buffalo wings. We'll wait for you to say it instead.

SERVES 8

1 (8-ounce) package **cream cheese**, room temperature

1 (10-ounce) can **chicken breast**, drained

1 teaspoon **onion powder**

1 teaspoon **garlic powder**

¼ cup diced **carrot**

¼ cup diced **celery**

½ cup **blue cheese dressing**

½ cup **buffalo wing sauce** (we like Frank's RedHot)

1 (8-ounce) bag **shredded cheddar cheese**

Baguette slices, for serving

1. Preheat the oven to 350°F with a rack in the center.

2. Spread cream cheese along the bottom of a 9-inch pie or baking dish. Layer on the chicken, onion powder, garlic powder, carrot, celery, blue cheese dressing, and wing sauce. Sprinkle the cheddar cheese over the top to cover.

3. Place the pie dish on a rimmed baking sheet. Bake the dip until the cheese is bubbling and starting to brown, 25 to 30 minutes.

4. Serve warm with a spoon and the baguette slices alongside.

TOUCHDOWN TIP: *Bake the dip in a 9-inch foil pie dish that's easy to store, transport, and reheat on the grill.*

SPINACH & ARTICHOKE BREAD BOWL

First of all, who doesn't love a bread bowl? Second, who doesn't love the spinach and artichoke combo?! This is the stuff of dreams, right here. You'll kick things off with some delicious croutons to get the dipping started. Then, as the dip level drops, the bread bowl will become the best-ever rip-and-tear situation.

SERVES 8

BREAD BOWL:

1 (10-inch) round **bread loaf**

2 tablespoon **extra-virgin olive oil**

4 tablespoons (½ stick) **unsalted butter**

½ teaspoon **garlic powder**

½ cup **shredded mozzarella cheese**

DIP:

4 tablespoons (½ stick) **unsalted butter**

4 **garlic cloves**, minced

2 (14-ounce) cans quartered **artichoke hearts**, drained and roughly chopped

1 (10-ounce) package **frozen spinach**, thawed and drained

½ teaspoon **kosher salt**, plus more as needed

½ teaspoon **freshly ground black pepper**, plus more as needed

½ teaspoon **red pepper flakes**

1 cup grated **Parmesan cheese**

1 (8-ounce) package **cream cheese**, room temperature

1. Preheat the oven to 350°F with a rack in the center. Line a rimmed baking sheet with parchment paper.

2. **MAKE THE BREAD BOWL:** Cut a large circle out from the top of the loaf of bread. Scoop out the bread, leaving a 1-inch border around the edge and stopping about ½ inch from the bottom. Cut the removed bread into 1-inch cubes and transfer them to a large bowl. Add the olive oil and toss to coat. Set aside.

3. Place the butter in a small bowl and microwave on high until melted, 30 seconds to 1 minute. Whisk the garlic powder into the melted butter, then brush the inside and outside of the bread bowl with the butter. Sprinkle half of the mozzarella inside the bread bowl and press the other half around its rim. Place the bread bowl on the prepared baking sheet. Scatter the coated cubed bread around the bread bowl. Bake until the mozzarella is starting to brown and the croutons are golden brown, 15 to 20 minutes.

4. **MEANWHILE, MAKE THE DIP:** In a large skillet over medium heat, melt the butter. Stir in the garlic and cook for about 1 minute, until fragrant. Add the artichokes, spinach, salt, black pepper, and red pepper flakes. Cook, stirring often, until any liquid has almost evaporated, about 5 minutes.

5. Stir in the Parmesan until melted and combined, then add the cream cheese. Stir constantly as the cream cheese melts and creates a cohesive, creamy dip. Remove the skillet from the heat and taste for seasoning.

6. When the bread bowl and croutons are done, transfer the bread bowl to a serving platter and fill with the dip. Serve with the croutons alongside with toothpicks for dipping.

WARM RED PEPPER JELLY & BACON DIP

There's the rookie version of this combination, which is spooning some pepper jelly over cream cheese. Then there's the all-star version, which is baking everything until it's bubbling and warm and the bacon—yes, bacon—on top is crisp and salty. Who are you going to be?

SERVES 8

1 (8-ounce) package **cream cheese**, room temperature

1 cup **shredded pepper jack cheese**

1 (10.5-ounce) jar **hot pepper jelly**

4 strips **thick-cut bacon**, chopped

Snack crackers (we like Ritz), for serving

1. Preheat the oven to 350°F with a rack in the center.

2. Spread the cream cheese along the bottom of a 9-inch pie or baking dish. Sprinkle the pepper jack cheese over the top, then spoon on the jelly and smooth it into an even layer. Sprinkle the bacon over everything.

3. Place the pie dish on a rimmed baking sheet. Bake until the jelly is bubbling and the bacon is crisped, 15 to 20 minutes.

4. Serve warm with a spoon and crackers alongside.

TOUCHDOWN TIP: *Bake the dip in a 9-inch foil pie dish that's easy to store, transport, and reheat on the grill.*

BLOOMIN' GARLIC BREAD

With all the easy grabbing of the famous onion, plus all the warm and toasty of garlic bread, this is an app to the max. Make it at home and warm it up, or make it on the grill and serve it piping hot. It doesn't matter—just make sure you make it. And a dipping bowl of warm marinara on the side is never a bad idea.

SERVES 6

Nonstick cooking spray

1 (10-inch) round **bread loaf**

½ cup (1 stick) **unsalted butter**

2 **garlic cloves**, minced

1 teaspoon **dried parsley**

½ teaspoon **red pepper flakes**

1 cup **shredded Italian blend cheese**

2 tablespoons **pesto**

2 tablespoons **extra-virgin olive oil**

1. Preheat the oven to 350°F with a rack in the center. Line a rimmed baking sheet with foil and coat the foil with nonstick spray.

2. Working on the diagonal, cut the bread into 1-inch-wide strips, stopping 1 inch before the bottom of the loaf. Rotate the loaf and cut in the opposite direction to create a diamond pattern. Place the cut bread on the prepared baking sheet.

3. In a small skillet over medium heat, melt the butter. Whisk in the garlic, parsley, and red pepper flakes. Spoon the butter mixture over the bread, letting it drip into the crevices. Sprinkle the cheese over the bread and gently press it into the crevices, leaving some cheese on the surface.

4. Bake until the cheese is melted and the bread is toasted, 15 to 20 minutes.

5. Meanwhile, in a small bowl, whisk together the pesto and olive oil. As soon as the bread comes out of the oven, immediately drizzle the pesto mixture over the entire surface. Let the bread cool for about 10 minutes, until cool enough to touch but still warm, then serve.

TOUCHDOWN TIP: *To make this dish on the grill, prep the grill for medium direct/indirect heat (see page 17), place the baking sheet on the indirect grates, and cover. Grill for 10 to 15 minutes, until the cheese is melted and the bread is toasted.*

SPIRIT DEVILED EGGS

The picnic classic gets a spirited update that you can customize however you like. The yellow filling is exactly as tangy and delicious as you remember, but the whites are the perfect canvas for claiming your turf. With a big platter of these on the table, there'll be no doubt whose team you're on.

SERVES 6

6 **large eggs**, cold

3 tablespoons **mayonnaise**

1 tablespoon **yellow mustard**

½ teaspoon **onion powder**

½ teaspoon **ground turmeric**

¼ teaspoon **kosher salt**

¼ teaspoon **freshly ground black pepper**

White vinegar

Food coloring

Dried parsley and **paprika**, for serving

1. Fill a large bowl with ice and water.

2. Bring a large saucepan filled with water to a rolling boil over high heat. Use a ladle to carefully lower the eggs into the water one at a time. Cook for 10 minutes, then drain the eggs and rinse under cold water. Submerge the eggs in the bowl of cold water and set aside.

3. Meanwhile, in a small bowl, stir together the mayonnaise, mustard, onion powder, turmeric, salt, and pepper.

4. In separate small bowls, combine ½ cup cold water, 1 tablespoon vinegar, and 2 to 4 drops food coloring in each to create your team colors.

5. Working with one egg at a time, tap the shell on all sides and carefully peel it off. Run the peeled egg under cold water to ensure all the shell is off. Slice the egg in half lengthwise. Scoop the yolk into the bowl with the mayonnaise mixture. Place the whites into a bowl of dye.

6. Soak the egg whites in the food coloring for 8 to 10 minutes, flipping halfway through, or until your desired color is reached. Remove the eggs from the dye and pat dry with paper towels. Arrange the egg whites on a serving tray.

7. Meanwhile, use a spoon to mash and mix the yolks into the mayonnaise mixture to combine well. Spoon the filling into the bottom corner of a large resealable zip-top bag.

8. Snip the corner from the zip-top bag and pipe the yolk mixture into each egg half. Garnish with parsley and paprika before serving.

GRILLED CHEESE BUBBLE BREAD

A perfect grilled cheese is a masterpiece. Crunchy brown on the outside, warm and gooey in the middle, fully satisfying through and through. Oh, wait. That exactly describes these tiny grilled-cheese bites. It's as easy as slicing and stuffing some premade pizza dough—in just a flash, you'll have enough cheesy goodness to serve a crowd.

SERVES 8

Vegetable oil, for greasing

1½ cups **shredded cheddar cheese**

8 strips **thick-cut bacon**, cooked and crumbled

1 tablespoon **dried chives**

½ teaspoon **freshly ground black pepper**

1 pound **frozen pizza dough**, thawed

All-purpose flour

8 slices **American cheese**, quartered

4 tablespoons (½ stick) **unsalted butter**, melted

2 tablespoons grated **Parmesan cheese**

1. Preheat the oven to 400°F with a rack in the center. Use a paper towel to grease a 9-inch cast-iron skillet or an 8 × 8-inch baking pan with vegetable oil.

2. In a small bowl, stir together the cheddar cheese, bacon, chives, and pepper.

3. Divide the dough into 16 equal-size pieces. On a lightly floured surface, roll out one piece of dough into a roughly 3-inch circle. Place a quarter piece of American cheese in the center along with a heaping tablespoon of the cheddar mixture. Fold the edges together, pinch tightly to enclose the filling, and place it in the prepared skillet. Repeat with the remaining dough and cheese. Brush about half of the melted butter over the dough balls.

4. Bake for 20 to 25 minutes, or until the tops are golden brown. Remove from the oven, brush with the remaining butter, and sprinkle the Parmesan over the top. Let cool in the skillet for about 10 minutes before serving.

TOUCHDOWN TIPS: *Bags of pre-shredded cheese are coated in powders to prevent sticking. Buy a block of cheese and shred it yourself for the most melt.*

To make this on the grill, prep the grill for medium direct/indirect heat (see page 17), place the skillet on the indirect grates, and cover. Grill for 15 to 20 minutes, until the buns are toasted.

MOZZARELLA HUSHPUPPIES

Welcome to the mash-up you didn't know you needed: mozzarella sticks and hushpuppies, two of the greatest starting players of all time. These stringy, gooey, and crispy-coated mozzapuppies (husharellas?) can and do stand proudly beside the original two. Make sure to serve with marinara *and* tartar sauce, because your taste buds will want both.

SERVES 6

1 (8.5-ounce) box **corn muffin mix**

¼ cup **all-purpose flour**

1 cup **whole milk**

1 large **egg**

½ teaspoon **kosher salt**, plus more as needed

½ teaspoon **freshly ground black pepper**

1 (8-ounce) container **mozzarella balls**, drained and pat dry

1 quart **vegetable oil**

Marinara and **tartar sauce**, for serving

1. In a large bowl, whisk together the muffin mix, flour, milk, egg, salt, and pepper. Fold in the mozzarella balls to coat. Cover and refrigerate for about 30 minutes, until the batter is thick.

2. Meanwhile, in a medium saucepan, heat the oil to 350°F. (Clip a deep-fry thermometer to the side of the saucepan or use an instant-read thermometer to check the temp.)

3. Use a fork to rotate each mozzarella ball and thoroughly coat it in the batter once more. Working in batches to avoid overcrowding, gently lower the balls into the oil. Fry for 3 to 4 minutes, or until the hushpuppies are a deep golden brown. Transfer to paper towels and immediately sprinkle with a pinch of salt. Repeat with the remaining mozzarella balls, allowing the oil to return to 350°F between batches.

4. Serve with the sauces alongside for dipping.

TAILGATE FRIES

You've heard of disco fries, chili cheese fries, and poutine. Enter Tailgate Fries, a mash-up of pretty much everything that's great about pregaming. We've got fries, obviously, plus barbecue pork, creamy coleslaw, and a smoky and spicy cheese sauce to top it all off. Bonus: up your game with waffle fries, tots, curly fries, or a combo of all of the above.

SERVES 6 TO 8

FRIES:

2 (28-ounce) bags **frozen crinkle-cut French fries**

1 pound **pulled pork**, store-bought or homemade *(see page 112)*

2 cups **barbecue sauce**, store-bought or homemade *(see page 118)*, plus more for serving

4 **scallions**, thinly sliced, for serving

COLESLAW:

½ cup **mayonnaise**

2 tablespoons **sugar**

2 tablespoons **white wine vinegar**

1 teaspoon **freshly ground black pepper**

½ teaspoon **celery salt**

1 (14-ounce) bag **coleslaw mix**

CHEESE SAUCE:

½ cup **whole milk**

16 slices **American cheese**

1 (4-ounce) jar **diced pimientos**, drained

1 teaspoon **smoked paprika**

1 teaspoon **hot sauce** (we like Tabasco)

1. **MAKE THE FRIES:** Bake the French fries according to the package directions. Meanwhile, add the pulled pork and BBQ sauce to a medium saucepan, cover, and cook over low heat, until the pork is warmed through, about 10 minutes. Keep warm over low heat until ready to use.

2. **MAKE THE COLESLAW:** In a medium bowl, whisk together the mayonnaise, sugar, vinegar, pepper, and celery salt until well combined. Fold in the coleslaw mix and toss to coat. Set aside.

3. **NEXT, MAKE THE CHEESE SAUCE:** Add the milk and cheese to a small saucepan over medium heat, stirring occasionally, until the cheese has melted, about 6 minutes. Stir in the pimientos, paprika, and hot sauce. Reduce the heat to low and keep warm until ready to use.

4. Divide the fries among the plates, then top each with pork and coleslaw. Spoon some cheese sauce on top and garnish with scallions to serve.

TOUCHDOWN TIP: *To make this on the grill, prepare the pork, coleslaw, and cheese sauce ahead of time. Prep the grill for medium direct/indirect heat (see page 17). Arrange the fries on a baking sheet, place on the indirect grates, cover, and grill until the fries are toasted, 20 to 25 minutes. Place the separate saucepans of pork and cheese sauce on the top rack to reheat while the fries bake.*

OVERTIME SNACK MIX

We all know how easy it is to get sucked in by the snack mix. Every salty bite makes you want more and more, until you've just about eaten the whole bowl yourself. These are our favorite snacks to mix, but anything cheesy, salty, and/or crunchy is a good move. This giant batch is guaranteed to hold up with even the most serious snackers around; just make sure to scatter some bowls around the party to avoid traffic jams.

SERVES 12

1 (16-ounce) bag **miniature pretzels**

1 (14-ounce) box **wheat Chex cereal**

1 (10-ounce) can **salted mixed nuts**

1 (7.2-ounce) bag **everything bagel chips**

1 (7-ounce) box **Cheez-It crackers**

1 (6-ounce) bag **Goldfish crackers**

1 (1-ounce) packet **ranch seasoning**

½ cup (1 stick) **unsalted butter**, melted

1. Divide the pretzels, cereal, nuts, bagel chips, and both crackers between two large microwave-safe bowls. In a small bowl, whisk the ranch seasoning and melted butter until well combined, then drizzle it evenly over both bowls. Using your hands, gently toss to coat.

2. Working with one bowl at a time, microwave on high for 6 minutes, stopping every 2 minutes to gently stir the mixture with a rubber spatula. Remove from the microwave and spread out on a flat paper towel–lined surface to cool.

3. Store in large zip-top bags until ready to serve.

ANTIPASTI SKEWERS

For something lighter, fresher, and, dare we say, kind of elegant, turn to these skewers. Adding tortellini to the skewers elevates the whole game, and a long soak in an herby marinade makes everything better. And, hey, a little advice: A pitcher of the Perfect Bloody *(see page 176)* doesn't hurt either.

===== MAKES 12 SKEWERS =====

1 (9-ounce) package **cheese tortellini**

½ cup **extra-virgin olive oil**

1 teaspoon **dried parsley**

1 teaspoon **dried basil**

1 teaspoon **dried oregano**

1 teaspoon **dried chives**

1 teaspoon **garlic powder**

1 teaspoon **onion powder**

½ teaspoon **red pepper flakes**

1 (8-ounce) container **mozzarella balls**, drained

1 (8-ounce) jar **sun-dried tomatoes**, drained

1 (5.75-ounce) jar **pimiento-stuffed olives**, drained

1 (4-ounce) package sliced **sandwich pepperoni**

1 (4-ounce) package sliced **hard salami**

1. Bring a large pot of water to a boil over high heat. Cook the tortellini according to package directions.

2. Meanwhile, add the oil, parsley, basil, oregano, chives, garlic powder, onion powder, and red pepper flakes to a large bowl and whisk until well combined. Fold in the mozzarella, sun-dried tomatoes, and olives.

3. When the tortellini is done, drain thoroughly and immediately add it to the bowl. Fold in the tortellini, then cover the bowl with plastic wrap and refrigerate for at least 2 hours and up to 24 hours.

4. Make each skewer with a combination of the marinated ingredients, pepperoni, and salami. Arrange the skewers on a rimmed baking sheet, cover with plastic wrap, and refrigerate until ready to serve.

WALKING TACOS

You might think of tacos as being hard to eat, but these convenient little treats come in a mess-free bag. Fritos are the classic move, but any snack pack of crunchy corn chips can sub in an emergency. The chili mix and cheese sauce can simmer away at the same time, making this an easy game-day option, whether you're on the couch or at the stadium.

SERVES 8

TACOS:

1 tablespoon **extra-virgin olive oil**

1 pound **ground beef**

1 large **yellow onion**, diced

1 (1.25-ounce) packet **chili seasoning**

1 (14.5-ounce) can **diced tomatoes**

1 (15.5-ounce) can **pinto beans**, drained and rinsed

½ teaspoon **kosher salt**

8 (1-ounce) bags **Fritos**

CHEESE SAUCE:

½ cup **whole milk**

16 slices **American cheese**

1 (7-ounce) can **sliced pickled jalapeños**, drained

FOR SERVING:

4 **scallions**, thinly sliced

1 large **white onion**, diced

2 cups **shredded cheddar cheese**

1. **MAKE THE TACOS:** Heat the oil in a large skillet over medium heat. When the oil is shimmering, add the beef and cook, breaking it up with a wooden spoon, until browned, about 6 minutes. Add the onion and chili seasoning and stir to combine, then add the tomatoes, beans, and salt. Reduce the heat to low and simmer for about 10 minutes.

2. **MEANWHILE, MAKE THE CHEESE SAUCE:** Add the milk and cheese to a small saucepan. Cook over medium heat, stirring occasionally, until the cheese has melted, about 6 minutes. Stir in the jalapeños. Reduce the heat to low and keep warm until ready to use.

3. Cut the top off the Fritos bags, then scoop ½ cup of the chili mixture into each one. Spoon some cheese sauce over top and garnish with scallions, onion, and cheese to serve.

TOUCHDOWN TIP: *To make this on the grill, prepare all the elements ahead of time. Warm the chili and cheese sauce on the top rack of a grill for 5 to 10 minutes—perfect if you have something else to cook on the grates below.*

GRILLED
JALAPEÑO POPPERS

Imagine a classic jalapeño popper, stuffed with oozing cheese and a little kick of spice, but then wrap it in crispy bacon. Yeah, perfection. This popper gets cooked on the grill until that bacon is crispy and the jalapeño is saturated in salty, delicious drippings. What we're saying is, there's no excuse not to make these.

=============================== SERVES 6 ===============================

1 (8-ounce) package **cream cheese**, room temperature

1 cup **shredded pepper jack cheese**

1 **garlic clove**, minced

¼ teaspoon **kosher salt**

¼ teaspoon **freshly ground black pepper**

12 **jalapeños**

12 strips **thick-cut bacon**

1. Preheat the grill to medium *(see page 17)*.

2. In a medium bowl, add the cream cheese, pepper jack, garlic, salt, and black pepper and stir to combine.

3. Cut the jalapeños in half lengthwise, keeping the halves paired together, and use a spoon to remove the seeds and veins. Fill one half of each pair with a spoonful of the cheese mixture, then place the matching half on top and wrap the entire jalapeño in a strip of bacon. Hold the bacon and jalapeño together with a toothpick to keep everything in place.

4. Grill the jalapeños, rotating occasionally, until the bacon is crisp and the jalapeños are cooked through, about 10 minutes.

PARTY TIME POTATO SKINS

For a spud-tacular app, there's nothing better than the dream team: twice-baked potatoes and potato skins. Crispy skins are the perfect vessel for all the creamy goodness of the fluffy mashed potato filling, which gets topped off with some melty cheddar and crispy bacon. Man, it's like they were meant to be best spuddies all along.

SERVES 8 TO 12

4 large **Russet potatoes** (about 1½ pounds)

¼ cup **extra-virgin olive oil**

2½ teaspoons **kosher salt**

½ cup **whole milk**

½ cup **sour cream**

1 tablespoon grated **Parmesan cheese**

1 tablespoon **dried chives**, plus more for serving

½ teaspoon **freshly ground black pepper**

8 strips **thick-cut bacon**, cooked and crumbled

1½ cups **shredded cheddar cheese**

1. Preheat the oven to 400°F with a rack in the center. Line a rimmed baking sheet with foil.

2. Poke the potatoes all over with a fork. Rub the skins with the oil and season with 1½ teaspoons of the salt. Place in a microwave-safe dish and microwave for about 7 minutes, flipping halfway through, until fork-tender. Test the potatoes for doneness and continue to microwave in 2-minute increments until done. Slice the potatoes in half lengthwise and set aside for about 30 minutes, or until cool enough to handle.

3. Meanwhile, add the milk, sour cream, Parmesan, chives, pepper, and remaining 1 teaspoon salt to a large bowl and whisk until well combined. Using a spoon, scoop most of the potato flesh out of the skins and into the large bowl, leaving about a ½-inch border of potato on all sides. Mash the scooped-out potato and other ingredients with a potato masher until it forms a cohesive, slightly lumpy texture.

4. Arrange the potato skins on the prepared baking sheet and fill each skin with the potato mixture, about two heaping spoonfuls per skin. Sprinkle them evenly with bacon and cheddar cheese. Transfer to the oven and bake for 15 to 20 minutes, until the cheese is melted and the potatoes are warmed through. Let rest on the baking sheet for about 10 minutes, or until cool enough to handle, then cut each potato into thirds, arrange them on a serving tray, and garnish with dried chives to serve.

TOUCHDOWN TIP: *To make this on the grill, prepare all the elements ahead of time. Prep the grill for medium direct/indirect heat (see page 17). Fill and arrange the potato skins on a baking sheet, place it on the indirect grates, cover, and grill over indirect heat until the cheese is melted, 10 to 15 minutes.*

PEPPERONI PIZZA BITES

When we say "Pepperoni Pizza," we really mean "Do Whatever You Want." Hawaiian, extra cheese, meat bonanza—you name it. But there is something about a classic pep pie that just hits different. Sliced in two directions, the pizza becomes a variety of bite-size shapes and textures (all crust, some crust, no crust) for a new experience each time you come back for more.

SERVES 6 TO 8

2 tablespoons **extra-virgin olive oil**

1 pound **frozen pizza dough**, thawed

1 cup **marinara sauce**

1 cup **shredded mozzarella cheese**

½ small **red onion**, thinly sliced

½ **green bell pepper**, thinly sliced

12 **pepperoni slices**

1. Preheat the oven to 450°F with a rack in the upper third. Rub a large oven-safe skillet with the oil.

2. Stretch the crust to fit the skillet and press it into the bottom and to the edges. Spread the marinara over the dough, leaving a 1-inch crust around the edge. Sprinkle with mozzarella and scatter with onions and bell pepper, then arrange the pepperoni on top.

3. Transfer the skillet to the oven and bake for about 20 minutes, or until the crust is golden and the cheese is melted. Cool for at least 10 minutes in the skillet, then transfer to a cutting board. Using a knife or pizza cutter, cut the pizza into squares with three long slices in one direction, then three more in the other direction. Serve immediately.

TOUCHDOWN TIP: *To make this on the grill, prep the grill for high direct/indirect heat (see page 17), then place the skillet on the indirect grates and cover. Grill over indirect heat for about 10 minutes, or until the bottom of the crust is set, then transfer the skillet to the upper rack, cover, and grill for 5 to 10 minutes more, until the crust is golden brown and the mozzarella is starting to caramelize.*

MINI MEATBALL SUBS

Toasted buns, perfect meatballs, pesto, marinara, gooey provolone. The vibes couldn't be more immaculate. These mini subs can be thrown together almost as fast as they disappear, so they're perfect for groups of all sizes. The best part? You can make the meatballs and sauce the night before—they always taste better the next day, anyway. That's just facts.

SERVES 6 TO 8

12 **Hawaiian sweet rolls**

1 pound **ground beef**

1 **large egg**, beaten

½ cup **seasoned breadcrumbs**

3 tablespoons **pesto**

1 teaspoon **kosher salt**

1 tablespoon **extra-virgin olive oil**

1 cup **marinara sauce**

4 slices **provolone cheese**

4 tablespoons (½ stick) **unsalted butter**, melted

1 teaspoon **onion powder**

1 teaspoon **garlic powder**

1 teaspoon **dried oregano**

½ teaspoon **red pepper flakes**

2 tablespoons grated **Parmesan cheese**

1. Preheat the oven to 350°F with a rack in the center. Line a rimmed baking sheet with parchment paper.

2. Keeping the rolls attached, slice laterally to create a group of top and bottom buns. Lay the halves on the prepared baking sheet, cut-sides up, and bake for about 15 minutes, or until the buns are golden brown and firm.

3. Meanwhile, add the beef, egg, breadcrumbs, pesto, and salt to a medium bowl and mix with your hands until well combined, then divide and shape into 12 meatballs.

4. Heat the oil in a large saucepan over medium-high heat. When the oil is shimmering, add the meatballs and brown for about 2 minutes per side. Add the marinara and ½ cup water and bring to a simmer, then reduce the heat to medium-low and simmer until the sauce is reduced by half and the meatballs are cooked through, about 5 minutes.

5. Spoon the meatballs and sauce over the toasted bun bottoms, top with the provolone, and add the top buns. Add the butter, onion powder, garlic powder, oregano, and red pepper flakes to a small bowl and whisk until well combined. Brush the tops of the buns with the butter mixture and sprinkle with the Parmesan. Bake until the provolone has melted and the buns are lightly browned, about 10 minutes.

6. Let the sandwiches cool on the baking sheet for 10 minutes, then transfer them to a serving platter. Let each person pull their own slider from the group.

TOUCHDOWN TIP: *To make this on the grill, prepare all the components ahead of time. Prep the grill for medium direct/indirect heat (see page 17) and assemble the sliders. Place the baking sheet on the indirect grates, cover, and grill over indirect heat for about 10 minutes, until the cheese has melted and the meatballs are warmed through.*

BLT BISCUITS

Whoever invented the BLT is literally a genius. The holy trinity is right in the name, of course, plus we can't forget the warm, toasty bread and tangy mayo that round out the trio. But like every coach will tell you, you can't rest on your laurels. So, in that spirit, let's substitute some buttery biscuits and bench the tomato in favor of a sweet and spiced tomato jam. These pumped-up BLTs are ready for the big time! Equally excellent warm or at room temp, they can be served right away or packed up for later.

SERVES 8

1 (16.3-ounce) can **biscuit dough**

8 strips **thick-cut bacon**

8 tablespoons **tomato jam**, store-bought or homemade *(recipe follows)*

8 tablespoons **mayonnaise**

2 cups **shredded iceberg** or **romaine lettuce**

1. Preheat the oven to 350°F with one rack in the center and one in the lower third. Line one rimmed baking sheet with parchment paper and another with foil.

2. Open the biscuit can and arrange the biscuits on the parchment-lined baking sheet, leaving 2 inches of space between them. Arrange the bacon on the foil-lined baking sheet. Place the biscuits on the center rack and the bacon on the lower rack and bake for 13 to 15 minutes, flipping the bacon strips halfway through, until the biscuits are golden and the bacon is crispy. Remove from the oven and transfer the bacon to a paper towel–lined plate. Let the biscuits cool on the baking sheet.

3. To assemble the BLTs, cut the biscuits in half laterally and spread 1 tablespoon of the tomato jam on each bottom half and 1 tablespoon of mayonnaise on each top half. Break a piece of bacon in half and arrange the pieces over the tomato jam in an X shape. Pile ¼ cup of the lettuce over the bacon, then press the top half down and secure it with a toothpick. Repeat with the remaining biscuits.

4. Serve warm or at room temperature.

Tomato Jam

2½ pounds **Roma tomatoes**, quartered and seeds removed

½ cup (packed) **dark brown sugar**

¼ cup **granulated sugar**

2 tablespoons **apple cider vinegar**

1 teaspoon **kosher salt**

½ teaspoon **freshly ground black pepper**

½ teaspoon **ground cumin**

½ teaspoon **smoked paprika**

¼ teaspoon **ground cloves**

Add the tomatoes, brown sugar, granulated sugar, vinegar, salt, pepper, cumin, paprika, and cloves to a large saucepan or Dutch oven and bring to a simmer over medium-high heat, stirring occasionally. Once simmering, reduce the heat to medium and cook, stirring occasionally, for about 2 hours, or until the mixture is thick and jammy. To test, scrape a wooden spoon through the jam. If the line holds, your jam is ready. (If not, keep cooking and checking every 10 to 15 minutes.)

Remove from the heat and cool in the pan for 30 minutes. Spoon the cooled jam into a pint jar or medium airtight container. Store in the refrigerator for up to 2 weeks.

JUICY LUCY SLIDERS

There are cheeseburgers and then there are *cheeseburgers*. Thanks to Minneapolis, we get to enjoy the latter. Instead of laying a slice on top of the patty, the Juicy Lucy has cheese stuffed *inside* the patty for gooey goodness in every bite. And, speaking of bites, these two-bite sliders are the perfect little snack to warm up for a big day of eating. Add a swipe of the most perfect Burger Sauce, and sandwich it all in a bun. P.S. You'll want to eat the Burger Sauce on basically everything, so make a big batch!

====== SERVES 6 TO 8 ======

2 pounds **ground beef**

1 tablespoon **Worcestershire sauce**

1 teaspoon **kosher salt**

½ teaspoon **freshly ground black pepper**

8 slices **American cheese**

1 tablespoon **vegetable oil**

12 **Hawaiian sweet rolls** or slider rolls

Burger Sauce, store-bought or homemade
(recipe follows) **special sauce**

Shredded iceberg lettuce, for serving

Dill pickle slices, for serving

1. Add the beef, Worcestershire sauce, salt, and pepper to a large bowl and combine using your hands, then divide and shape it into 12 equal-size balls.

2. Cut the cheese slices in half, then fold each half in half. Press a folded cheese piece into the center of each ball and roll between your hands to seal. Press each ball into a patty about ½ inch thick.

3. Heat the oil in a large skillet over medium heat. When the oil is shimmering, swirl to coat the skillet. Working in batches, sear the burgers for about 3 minutes per side, or until the burgers are browned and cooked to 160°F (for medium).

4. Place the cooked patties on the rolls and top with Burger Sauce, lettuce, and pickles to serve.

TOUCHDOWN TIP: *Since the burgers are small, heat a skillet over direct heat on the grill instead of cooking them directly on the grates.*

Burger Sauce

MAKES 1 CUP

½ cup **mayonnaise**

3 tablespoons **ketchup**

2 tablespoons **sweet relish**

1 tablespoon **hot sauce**

1 tablespoon **onion powder**

1 tablespoon **smoked paprika**

In a small bowl, whisk the mayonnaise, ketchup, relish, hot sauce, onion powder, and paprika to combine. Store in an airtight container in the refrigerator for up to 1 week.

BBQ CHICKEN BITES

BBQ chicken has already conquered pizza, sandwiches, quesadillas, and wings. Now it's coming for the pizza rolls' turf. A mix of chicken, barbecue, and ranch (a must) fills a soft little pocket that gets covered in gooey cheese and dipped in more ranch (again, a must).

SERVES 10

Nonstick cooking spray

2 tablespoons **extra-virgin olive oil**

1 pound **ground chicken**

1 (1-ounce) packet **ranch seasoning**

½ cup **barbecue sauce**, store-bought or homemade *(see page 118)*

1 pound **frozen pizza dough**, thawed

2 tablespoons **unsalted butter**, melted

1 cup **shredded Mexican blend cheese**

Ranch dressing, for serving

1. Preheat the oven to 350°F with a rack in the center. Coat a large oven-safe skillet with nonstick spray. Set aside.

2. In a separate large skillet, heat the oil over medium-high heat. When the oil is shimmering, add the chicken and cook, breaking it up with a wooden spoon, 3 to 5 minutes, or until cooked through. Stir in the ranch seasoning and barbecue sauce and bring to a simmer. Cook, stirring occasionally, for about 3 minutes more, or until the sauce has thickened and the chicken is coated. Remove from the heat and set aside.

3. Roll the pizza dough into a 12 × 15-inch rectangle, then cut it into twenty 3 × 3-inch pieces. Add a heaping tablespoon of the chicken mixture to the center of each dough piece. Pull the corners together and pinch to seal shut.

4. Nestle the chicken bites into the prepared oven-safe skillet. Brush the tops with the melted butter, then transfer to the oven. Bake for about 20 minutes, or until the bites are golden brown and cooked through. Sprinkle the cheese over the top and bake for 5 minutes more, or until the cheese has melted and started to brown. Remove from the oven and cool in the skillet for 10 minutes before serving. Serve with ranch dressing.

TOUCHDOWN TIP: *Make these ahead and reheat the entire skillet on the top rack of a grill for 5 to 10 minutes while cooking something else on the grates below.*

SPICY HONEY WINGS

Sweet and spicy is a combo that can't be beat. Little-league wings might get brushed with a lazy glaze, but these babies get tossed in a mix of tangy lime, savory onion, sticky honey, and a kick of cayenne. Take our word for it: it's impossible to eat just one.

SERVES 6 TO 8

SPICY HONEY:

Juice of 2 **limes**

1 small **red onion**, halved and thinly sliced

1 teaspoon **kosher salt**

1 teaspoon **cayenne pepper**

½ cup **honey**

WINGS:

4 pounds **chicken wings**

2 tablespoons **vegetable oil**

2 tablespoons **kosher salt**

1 tablespoon **freshly ground black pepper**

2 tablespoons **honey**

FOR SERVING:

2 tablespoons thinly sliced **fresh chives**

1 tablespoon toasted **sesame seeds**

1. **MAKE THE SPICY HONEY:** In a large bowl, combine the lime juice, onion, and salt. Let rest for 5 minutes. Add the cayenne and honey and stir until well combined.

2. **MAKE THE WINGS:** In a separate large bowl, toss the wings with the oil, salt, and black pepper until evenly coated.

    To make the wings on the grill:

    Prep the grill for medium heat *(see page 17)*. Arrange the wings on the grill and cook uncovered for about 25 minutes, flipping every 5 minutes, until the skin is crisp and lightly charred.

    To make the wings in the oven:

    Preheat the oven to 400°F and set two racks in the center of the oven. Line two rimmed baking sheets with foil and coat with nonstick spray. Arrange the wings on the baking sheets and bake for about 45 minutes, rotating the baking sheets front to back halfway through, or until the skin is crisp and lightly charred.

    Transfer the cooked wings to the bowl with the spicy honey mixture and toss to coat. Transfer the wings to a serving plate, drizzle with the honey, and garnish with chives and sesame seeds. Serve immediately.

TOUCHDOWN TIP: *For unbelievably tender and flavorful wings, toss the chicken with the oil, salt, and black pepper, then cover tightly and refrigerate overnight. Bring them up to room temp before cooking.*

CHEESESTEAK QUESO-DILLA

Philly cheesesteak and cheesy quesadillas are perfect game-day foods, so why not combine them to make the ultimate fantasy team. Seared slices of steak, plus onions, peppers, and provolone, get folded in a tortilla. But because we live by "go big or go home," that tortilla also gets a slather of queso dip for a melting pool of cheese guaranteed to make grown men cry.

SERVES 8

1 pound **skirt steak**

Kosher salt and **freshly ground black pepper**

2 tablespoons **extra-virgin olive oil**

1 large **white onion**, halved and sliced

1 **green bell pepper**, cut into large strips

4 (10-inch) **flour tortillas**

1 cup **Queso Overload** (see page 35), **Beer Cheese** (see page 83), or store-bought **salsa con queso**, plus more for serving

8 slices **provolone cheese**

1. Season the steak on both sides with salt and black pepper. Heat the oil in a large skillet over medium-high heat. When the oil is shimmering, add the steak and sear for about 3 minutes on each side, until the internal temperature reads 160°F (for medium). Transfer the steak to a cutting board and cover it loosely with foil.

2. Meanwhile, add the onion and bell pepper to the same skillet and cook over medium-high heat for about 5 minutes, tossing occasionally, until tender and the onions are translucent, then transfer to a plate. Slice the steak against the grain into thin strips.

3. Add a tortilla to the same skillet, then spread 4 tablespoons of the queso evenly across the tortilla, add 2 slices of the provolone, and one-fourth of the steak, onions, and bell peppers. Fold the tortilla in half over itself and cook over medium heat for about 3 minutes per side, or until evenly toasted and the cheese is melted. Repeat with the remaining tortillas, queso, cheese, steak, and vegetables.

4. Cut each quesadilla into 4 pieces and serve with more queso for dipping.

TOUCHDOWN TIP: *Prep the grill for medium direct/indirect heat (see page 17). Add the steak to the grill and cook over indirect heat for 3 minutes on each side. The vegetables can also be grilled over indirect heat, and the queso-dilla can be made in a cast-iron skillet.*

CHEESY PIGS IN A BLANKET

Do pigs in a blanket *need* anything else to be one of the best appetizers of all time? Not really. Did we *want* to up the game with gooey American cheese and everything bagel seasoning? Oh yeah. All that's left to say is you're welcome!

SERVES 6 TO 8

1 (8-ounce) tube **crescent rolls**

8 **hot dogs**

8 slices **American cheese**

2 tablespoons **everything bagel seasoning**

Ketchup and **mustard**, for serving

1. Preheat the oven to 375°F with a rack in the center. Line a rimmed baking sheet with parchment paper.

2. Unroll the crescent dough and roll out the perforations. Use a knife or a pizza cutter to cut it lengthwise into 8 even strips, then cut the strips in half crosswise to make 16. Cut the hot dogs in half to make 16 mini dogs. Slice each square of cheese into 4 strips to make 32 strips. Add the everything bagel seasoning to a small plate.

3. Lay 2 strips of cheese over a piece of dough. Lay a mini dog on one side and roll to wrap it in the dough. Pinch the dough to seal tightly around the dog. Dip one side in the bagel seasoning and place on the prepared baking sheet, unseasoned-side down. Repeat with the remaining dough, cheese, dogs, and seasoning.

4. Transfer the baking sheet to the oven and bake for 12 to 15 minutes, until the dough is golden brown. Serve immediately with ketchup and mustard on the side.

TOUCHDOWN TIP: *Make these ahead and reheat the entire baking sheet on the top rack of a grill for 5 to 10 minutes while cooking something else on the grates below.*

LEMON PEPPER
POPCORN CHICKEN

Lemon pepper stans know what's up. This champion of seasonings is a surefire way to take your chicken game to the next level. And speaking of next-level, welcome to the world of double frying. It might seem excessive, but trust us: you've never had chicken this crispy.

SERVES 6

CHICKEN:

2 pounds **boneless, skinless chicken breast**, cut into 1-inch pieces

1 **large egg**, beaten

Zest and juice of 1 **lemon**

2 teaspoons **freshly ground black pepper**

2 teaspoons **kosher salt**

2 quarts **vegetable oil**

2 cups **cornstarch**

LEMON PEPPER SAUCE:

4 tablespoons (½ stick) **unsalted butter**, melted

Zest and juice of 1 **lemon**

1 tablespoon **freshly ground black pepper**

1 teaspoon **kosher salt**

1 teaspoon **onion powder**

1. **MAKE THE CHICKEN:** In a large bowl, combine the chicken, egg, lemon zest and juice, pepper, and salt. Cover with plastic wrap and refrigerate for at least 30 minutes and up to 1 hour.

2. Add the oil to a large Dutch oven or saucepan and bring to 350°F over medium-high heat. Add the cornstarch to the chicken ½ cup at a time, mixing with your hands until well combined before adding more.

3. Working in four batches, carefully lower the chicken into the hot oil. Fry until golden and crisp, about 5 minutes. Transfer each batch to paper towels to drain, and allow the oil temperature to again reach 350°F before frying the next batch.

4. Once all the chicken is fried, increase the oil temperature to 350°F again, then add half of the fried chicken to fry it a second time. Fry for about 5 minutes, until the chicken is deep brown and very crispy. Transfer to a paper towel–lined plate to cool while frying the remaining half.

5. **MEANWHILE, MAKE THE SAUCE:** In a large bowl, whisk together the butter, lemon zest and juice, pepper, salt, and onion powder until well combined. Add the fried chicken and toss to coat. Serve immediately.

TOUCHDOWN TIP: *Fry the chicken at home and let cool completely on paper towels before packing it in a large zip-top bag. Add the sauce to the bag and toss just before serving to keep the chicken crunchy.*

SOFT PRETZEL BITES
with BEER CHEESE

The path to homemade pretzel bites is as easy as thawing dough (okay, there are a few more steps, but the point is they're easy). For a sauce that's better than the local pub's and a flavor combo that can't be beat, this is a winning play every time.

===== SERVES 8 =====

1 pound **frozen pizza dough**, thawed

¼ cup **baking soda**

1 **large egg**

2 tablespoons **flaky sea salt**

Beer Cheese, store-bought or homemade
(recipe follows)

1. Preheat the oven to 425°F with a rack in the center. Line one rimmed baking sheet with parchment paper and another with paper towels.

2. Divide the dough into fourths. Roll each piece into a 1-inch-thick rope and cut it into 1-inch-long pieces.

3. Bring 2 quarts water to a rolling boil in a large Dutch oven over medium-high heat. When the water is boiling, add the baking soda, being careful not to let the water boil over. Add half of the dough pieces and boil until they're puffy and floating, about 1 minute. Transfer the cooked dough to the paper towel–lined baking sheet and repeat with the remaining dough.

4. In a small bowl, whisk the egg with 1 tablespoon water. Add the sea salt to a shallow bowl.

5. Dip each boiled dough piece first in the egg, let any excess drip off, then roll it in the salt. Arrange the prepared pieces on the parchment-lined baking sheet and transfer to the oven. Bake until the bites are deeply golden brown, about 15 minutes. Let cool on the baking sheet for about 30 minutes. Serve with Beer Cheese for dipping.

TOUCHDOWN TIP: *Make everything ahead of time. Reheat the saucepan of Beer Cheese on the top rack of a grill for 5 to 10 minutes while cooking something else on the grates below.*

Beer Cheese

MAKES 2½ CUPS

16 ounces **sharp cheddar cheese**

1 tablespoon **cornstarch**

1 (12-ounce) can **IPA** or **lager beer**

2 tablespoons **Worcestershire sauce**

1 tablespoon **hot sauce**

Grate the cheese into a medium bowl, using the large holes on a box grater. Add the cornstarch and toss to coat.

In a medium saucepan over medium heat, bring the beer, Worcestershire sauce, and hot sauce to a simmer. Add the cheese mixture, stir, and simmer, whisking often, for about 3 minutes, or until smooth. Continue whisking until the sauce starts to bubble and thicken, about 2 minutes more. Serve immediately. Leftovers can be refrigerated in an airtight container for up to 1 week.

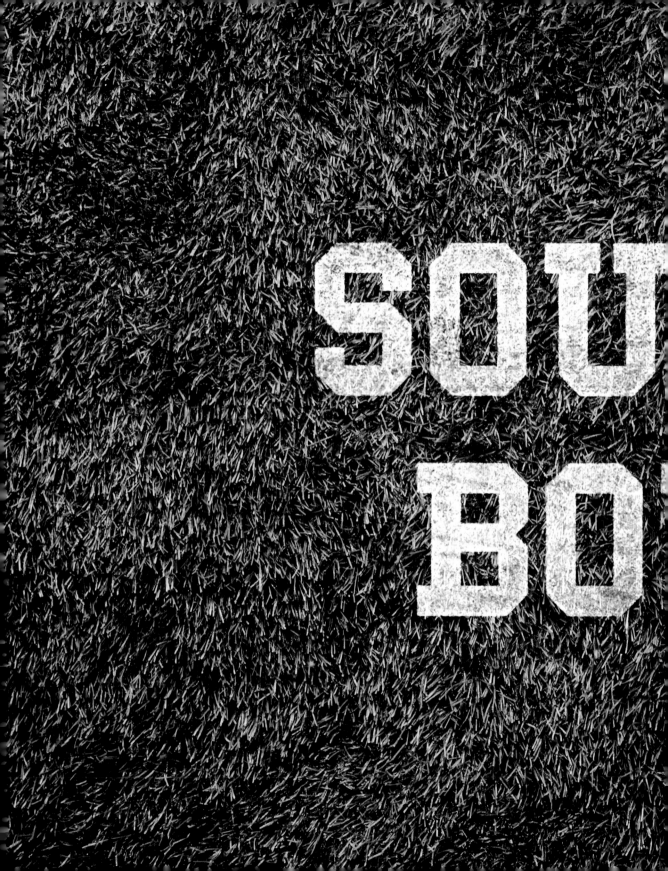

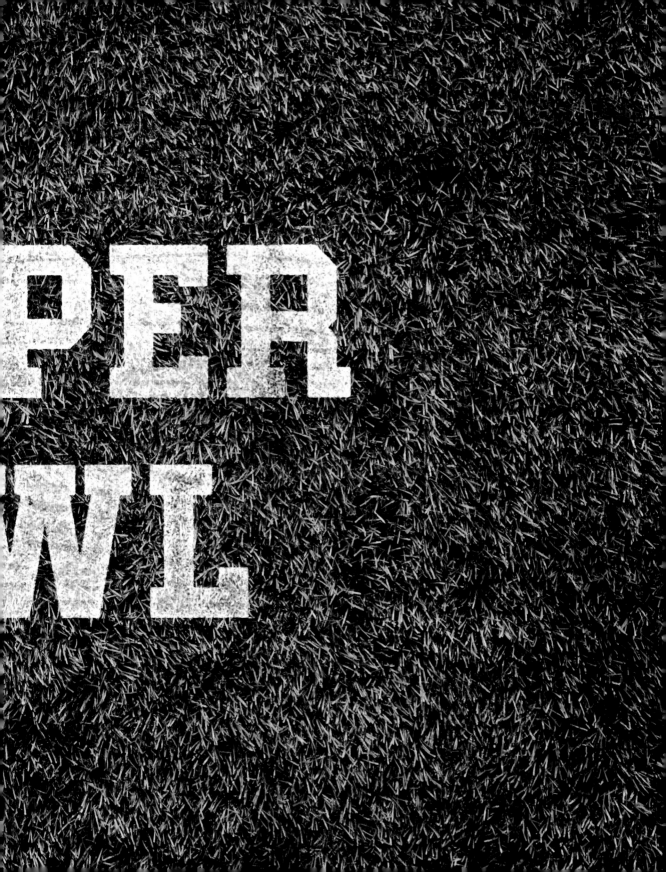

CHICKEN ALFREDO SOUP

This has all the creamy richness you expect from the classic pasta dish, but in a very downable bowl of soup. Chicken, broccoli, and noodles swirl around in a creamy broth for one satisfying spoonful after another. There will be no leftovers, we guarantee it.

SERVES 8 TO 10

2 pounds **boneless, skinless chicken breasts**

1½ teaspoons **kosher salt**

1 teaspoon **freshly ground black pepper**

2 tablespoons (¼ stick) **unsalted butter**

1 large **white onion**, finely chopped

2 **garlic cloves**, minced

¼ cup **all-purpose flour**

4 cups **chicken stock**

2 cups **half-and-half**

1 cup grated **Parmesan cheese**

4 cups **egg noodles**

2 cups **frozen broccoli**

1 teaspoon **red pepper flakes**

Dried parsley, for serving

1. Season the chicken with 1 teaspoon of the salt and ½ teaspoon of the black pepper. Melt the butter in a large Dutch oven over medium-high heat. Add the chicken and cook until golden and cooked through, about 6 minutes per side. Transfer the chicken to a large bowl.

2. Add the onion to the Dutch oven and cook for about 5 minutes, stirring frequently, until softened and translucent. Add the garlic and cook for 1 minute more, or until fragrant. Whisk in the flour and cook for about 2 minutes, whisking often, until the flour is golden brown and fragrant. Add the chicken stock, half-and-half, Parmesan, and the remaining ½ teaspoon salt and ½ teaspoon black pepper and stir to combine. Bring to a simmer, add the noodles, cover, and simmer for 8 to 10 minutes, until the noodles are al dente.

3. Meanwhile, use two forks to shred the chicken. Add the chicken, broccoli, and red pepper flakes to the Dutch oven and stir to combine. Simmer until the chicken and broccoli are warmed through, about 2 minutes. Divide the soup among bowls and garnish with parsley to serve.

TOUCHDOWN TIP: *Transfer the finished soup to a portable slow cooker to keep it toasty warm all day. This recipe is made for a 6-quart vessel (or larger).*

KENTUCKY BURGOO

A big pot of burgoo is historically a communal stew, meant to be made with whatever's on hand, served with cornbread, and shared with the people around you. Gathering together is still the defining principle of burgoo. So whip up a big batch and huddle up!

SERVES 8 TO 10

- 1 pound **boneless, skinless chicken thighs**, cut into 2-inch pieces
- 1 pound **boneless beef chuck**, cut into 2-inch pieces
- 2 pounds **boneless pork shoulder**, cut into 2-inch pieces
- 1 tablespoon plus 1 teaspoon **kosher salt**
- 1 teaspoon **freshly ground black pepper**
- 2 tablespoons **extra-virgin olive oil**, plus more as needed
- 2 medium **carrots**, diced
- 2 stalks **celery**, diced
- 1 **green bell pepper**, diced
- 1 large **yellow onion**, diced
- 4 **garlic cloves**, minced
- 2 tablespoons **Worcestershire sauce**
- 4 cups **chicken stock**
- 1 (28-ounce) can **crushed tomatoes**
- 1 pound **Russet potatoes**, cut into ½-inch pieces
- 2 cups **frozen corn**
- 2 cups **frozen lima beans**
- **Hot sauce**, for serving

1. Add the chicken, beef, and pork to a large bowl and season with 1 tablespoon of the salt and the black pepper. Heat the oil in a large Dutch oven over medium-high heat. When the oil is shimmering, add half of the meat and cook for about 6 minutes, flipping halfway through, until browned on both sides. Transfer to a plate and repeat with the remaining meat, adding more oil as needed.

2. Add the carrots, celery, bell pepper, onion, garlic, and Worcestershire sauce to the Dutch oven and cook until the vegetables have softened and are starting to brown, 8 to 10 minutes. Stir in the chicken stock and the remaining 1 teaspoon salt, scraping up any browned bits from the bottom of the Dutch oven. Add the tomatoes and the meat, plus any juices from the plate, and bring to a simmer, then cover and reduce the heat to medium-low. Cook for about 1 hour, stirring occasionally, or until the meat is tender. Return the meat to the plate.

3. Increase the heat to medium-high, return the soup to a simmer, and add the potatoes. Cover and simmer for about 20 minutes, or until the potatoes are fork-tender. Meanwhile, shred the meat.

4. Add the shredded meat, frozen corn, and lima beans to the Dutch oven. Cover and simmer for about 5 minutes, or until everything is warmed through. Divide the soup among bowls and serve with hot sauce.

TOUCHDOWN TIP: *Transfer the finished soup to a portable slow cooker to keep it toasty warm all day. This recipe is made for a 6-quart vessel (or larger).*

LOADED BAKED POTATO SOUP

No one eats a baked potato for the *potato*. It's all about the toppings, baby! This pot of soup has the butter, sour cream, and chives mixed right in. Top it with cheddar and bacon and you've got yourself a little bowl of perfection!

SERVES 8 TO 10

2 pounds **Russet potatoes**, cut into ½-inch pieces

2 tablespoons **extra-virgin olive oil**

1½ teaspoons **kosher salt**, plus more as needed

1½ teaspoons **freshly ground black pepper**

4 tablespoons (½ stick) **unsalted butter**

1 large **yellow onion**, finely chopped

2 **garlic cloves**, minced

⅓ cup **all-purpose flour**

2 cups **heavy cream**

¼ cup **sour cream**

¼ cup grated **Parmesan cheese**

4 cups **vegetable broth**

2 tablespoons **dried chives**, plus more for serving

Shredded cheddar cheese and chopped **bacon**, for serving

1. Preheat the oven to 450°F with a rack in the center.

2. Add the potatoes, olive oil, ½ teaspoon of the salt, and ½ teaspoon of the pepper to a rimmed baking sheet and toss to coat. Bake until the potatoes are fork-tender, about 20 minutes, then set aside.

3. Melt the butter in a large Dutch oven over medium heat. Add the onion and cook for about 5 minutes, stirring frequently, until softened and translucent. Add the garlic and cook for 1 minute more, or until fragrant.

4. Whisk in the flour and cook for about 2 minutes, whisking constantly, until the flour is golden brown and fragrant. Whisk in the heavy cream, sour cream, and Parmesan and simmer for about 2 minutes, or until the mixture begins to thicken. Add the vegetable broth, chives, and the remaining 1 teaspoon each salt and pepper. Bring to a boil, cover, and reduce the heat to low. Simmer for about 20 minutes, or until the flavors marry.

5. Using a rubber spatula or spoon, add the potatoes and their oil into the Dutch oven and stir to combine. Simmer, uncovered, for about 5 minutes more, or until the potatoes are warmed through.

6. Divide the soup among bowls and garnish with cheese, bacon, and more dried chives.

TOUCHDOWN TIP: *Transfer the finished soup to a portable slow cooker to keep it toasty warm all day. This recipe is made for a 6-quart vessel (or larger).*

SOUTHWEST CHILI VERDE

A staple of the American Southwest, a good chili verde features unbelievably tender chunks of pork swimming in a flavorful green salsa. The great news is that after getting everything going, you can just kick back and wait while it simmers away. You can even treat your grill like a stove *(see page 18 for tips on that)*—no matter how you do it, just be sure to serve it piping hot.

=== SERVES 8 TO 10 ===

SALSA VERDE:

2 cups **lager beer**

1 pound **fresh tomatillos**, husked and rinsed

1 large bunch **scallions**

3 packed cups **fresh cilantro**, leaves and tender stems

8 **garlic cloves**

1 tablespoon **ground cumin**

1 tablespoon **dried oregano**

1 tablespoon **kosher salt**

2 teaspoons **freshly ground black pepper**

CHILI:

2 tablespoons **extra-virgin olive oil**, plus more as needed

2 **poblano** or **Anaheim chiles**, seeded and chopped

1 large **white onion**, finely chopped

4 pounds **boneless pork shoulder**, cut into 2-inch pieces

2 teaspoons **kosher salt**

1 teaspoon **freshly ground black pepper**

FOR SERVING:

Sour cream

Chopped fresh cilantro

1. **MAKE THE SALSA VERDE:** Add the beer, tomatillos, scallions, cilantro, garlic, cumin, oregano, salt, and pepper to a blender and blend on high until a smooth sauce forms, about 1 minute.

2. **MAKE THE CHILI:** Heat the oil in a large Dutch oven over medium-high heat. When the oil is shimmering, stir in the chiles and onion and cook until softened, about 5 minutes.

3. Season the pork all over with the salt and pepper. Add half of the pork to the Dutch oven in an even layer and sear for about 4 minutes, flipping halfway through, until browned. Transfer to a plate and repeat with the remaining pork, adding more oil as needed. Add the pork and salsa verde to the Dutch oven and bring to a simmer. Once simmering, cover and reduce the heat to medium-low. Cook for 1 to 2 hours, or until the pork is falling apart. Remove from heat and use tongs or a wooden spoon to gently break the pork into bite-size pieces. Divide the chili among bowls and serve with sour cream and cilantro.

TOUCHDOWN TIP: *Transfer the finished soup to a portable slow cooker to keep it toasty warm all day. This recipe is made for a 6-quart vessel (or larger).*

TEXAS CHILI CON CARNE

Everything's bigger in Texas, including the flavor packed in this pot. Preparing the dried chiles might seem intimidating, but it's minimal work for maximum impact. Honestly, the hardest part is waiting for the beef to become melt-in-your-mouth tender. This recipe is perfectly suited for the grill, too *(see page 18 for tips on turning your grill into a stove)*.

=== SERVES 8 TO 10 ===

2 ounces **dried ancho** or **guajillo chiles**

2 tablespoons **vegetable oil**, plus more as needed

2 pounds **boneless beef chuck**, cut into 2-inch pieces

2 teaspoons **kosher salt**

1 teaspoon **freshly ground black pepper**

1 large **white onion**, quartered

2 **garlic cloves**

2 packed tablespoons **dark brown sugar**

2 tablespoons **apple cider vinegar**

2 teaspoons **ground cumin**

1 quart **beef stock**

FOR SERVING:

Sour cream

Lime wedges

1. Add the chiles to a large Dutch oven over medium heat. Toast until fragrant, about 2 minutes per side. Transfer the chiles to a large bowl and top with hot water, then cover with plastic wrap and soak for 15 minutes.

2. While the chiles soak, add the oil to the same Dutch oven over medium heat. Season the beef all over with 1 teaspoon of the salt and the pepper. When the oil is shimmering, add half of the beef in a single, even layer. Sear for about 2 minutes, or until browned, then flip and sear for 2 minutes more. Transfer to a plate and repeat with the remaining beef, adding more oil as needed. Remove the Dutch oven from the heat and return all the beef to the pot.

3. Once the chiles are pliable, remove the stems and seeds. Add the chiles, onion, garlic, brown sugar, vinegar, cumin, the remaining 1 teaspoon salt, and the beef stock to a blender. Blend on high until smooth, about 1 minute. Pour into the Dutch oven with the beef.

4. Return the Dutch oven to high heat and bring to simmer, then cover, reduce the heat to medium-low, and cook for 1 to 2 hours, or until the beef is tender. Divide the chili among bowls and top with sour cream and lime wedges to serve.

TOUCHDOWN TIP: *Transfer the finished soup to a portable slow cooker to keep it toasty warm all day. This recipe is made for a 6-quart vessel (or larger).*

CAJUN GUMBO

An absolute staple of Creole cooking, gumbo marries the holy trinity of veggies—onion, celery, and bell peppers—with the holy trinity of meats—chicken, sausage, and shrimp. Perfectly seasoned and soaking into a bowl of rice, it's a dish that will warm you to the core.

SERVES 8 TO 10

2 tablespoons **extra-virgin olive oil**

2 pounds **boneless, skinless chicken thighs**, cut into 1-inch pieces

2 tablespoons **Cajun seasoning**

1 teaspoon **freshly ground black pepper**

1 teaspoon **garlic powder**

1 teaspoon **smoked paprika**

1 teaspoon **cayenne pepper**

2 teaspoons **kosher salt**

8 cooked **andouille sausages**, sliced into ½-inch-thick rounds

4 stalks **celery**, diced

2 **green bell peppers**, diced

2 large **yellow onions**, diced

8 **garlic cloves**, minced

4 tablespoons (½ stick) **unsalted butter**

⅓ cup **all-purpose flour**

4 cups **chicken stock**

2 cups **frozen okra**

1 pound **jumbo shrimp**, peeled and deveined

Cooked **white rice**, for serving

Thinly sliced **scallions**, for serving

Hot sauce, for serving

1. Heat 1 tablespoon of the oil in a large Dutch oven over medium-high heat. When the oil is shimmering, add the chicken, Cajun seasoning, black pepper, garlic powder, paprika, cayenne, and 1 teaspoon of the salt, and stir to combine. Cook for about 5 minutes, or until the meat is nicely browned all over, then add the sausages and cook for 3 to 4 more minutes, until the chicken is cooked through and the sausage is warmed. Transfer the chicken and sausage to a large plate.

2. Add the remaining 1 tablespoon oil to the Dutch oven, along with the celery, bell peppers, onion, garlic, and the remaining 1 teaspoon salt and cook until the vegetables have softened and are starting to brown, 8 to 10 minutes. Add the butter and stir to melt, then add the flour. Continue stirring until the flour is a rich brown and very fragrant, about 5 minutes.

3. Stir in the chicken stock, scraping up any browned bits from the bottom of the Dutch oven. Return the chicken and sausages to the pot along with any collected juices. Add the okra, bring the liquid to a simmer, then reduce the heat to low, cover, and simmer for about 10 minutes, until the gumbo is bubbling and the flavors are fully married. Stir in the shrimp, cover, and simmer for about 5 minutes more, until the shrimp is just opaque. Divide the rice among bowls, top with a big scoop of gumbo, and garnish with scallions and hot sauce to serve.

TOUCHDOWN TIP: *Transfer the finished soup to a portable slow cooker to keep it toasty warm all day. This recipe is made for a 6-quart vessel (or larger).*

CHICKEN TORTILLA SOUP

The tortilla topping in Chicken Tortilla Soup is obviously the best part, but that's no excuse to slack off on the rest of the soup. Bites of tender chicken are accompanied by green chiles, beans, and corn—maybe even a swirl of sour cream—all in a super-flavorful broth.

SERVES 8 TO 10

2 tablespoons **extra-virgin olive oil**

1 large **white onion**, chopped

2 **garlic cloves**, minced

½ teaspoon **dried oregano**

½ teaspoon **ground cumin**

½ teaspoon **chili powder**

1 teaspoon **kosher salt**

1 teaspoon **freshly ground black pepper**

4 cups **chicken stock**

1 pound **boneless, skinless chicken breasts**

1 (14.5-ounce) can **diced tomatoes**

2 (4-ounce) cans **diced green chiles**

2 (15.5-ounce) cans **black beans**, drained and rinsed

2 cups frozen **corn**

FOR SERVING:

Sour cream

Crushed **tortilla chips**

Fresh cilantro leaves

Lime wedges

1. Heat the oil in a large Dutch oven over medium heat. When the oil is shimmering, add the onion and cook, stirring occasionally, for about 5 minutes, or until soft. Stir in the garlic, oregano, cumin, and chili powder and cook for about 30 seconds more, until fragrant.

2. Add the salt, pepper, and stock and increase the heat to medium-high. When the mixture begins to boil, add the chicken breasts, then reduce the heat to low and cover. Simmer for 8 to 10 minutes, until the chicken is cooked through. Transfer the chicken to a plate to rest.

3. Add the tomatoes, green chiles, black beans, and corn to the broth. Cook, stirring occasionally, until all the ingredients are heated through, about 5 minutes. Shred the chicken with two forks and return it to the soup along with any collected juices. Cook for about 5 more minutes to marry the flavors.

4. Divide the soup among bowls and serve with a dollop of sour cream, tortilla chips, cilantro, and a lime wedge.

TOUCHDOWN TIP: *Transfer the finished soup to a portable slow cooker to keep it toasty warm all day. This recipe is made for a 6-quart vessel (or larger).*

NEW ENGLAND
CLAM CHOWDER

There's Manhattan, Long Island, and Rhode Island, but the MVP of clam chowder is, hands down, New England—the warmest and most comforting of them all. Creamy and rich, with just enough briny ocean flavors, this is the perfect cure for a chilly day.

SERVES 8 TO 10

- 8 strips **thick-cut bacon**, chopped
- 2 tablespoons (¼ stick) **unsalted butter**, room temperature
- 4 stalks **celery**, chopped
- 1 large **white onion**, chopped
- 2 **garlic cloves**, minced
- ⅓ cup **all-purpose flour**
- 1 teaspoon **freshly ground black pepper**, plus more for serving
- 1 teaspoon **dried thyme**

- 1 tablespoon **kosher salt**
- 1 pound **Russet potatoes**, cut into ½-inch cubes
- 4 (8-ounce) bottles **clam juice**
- 4 cups **chicken stock**
- 4 cups **half-and-half**
- 4 (6.5-ounce) cans **chopped clams**, drained
- Chopped **fresh chives**, for serving
- **Oyster crackers**, for serving

1. Add the bacon to a large Dutch oven over medium heat. Cook, stirring occasionally, until the fat renders and the bacon is crisp, about 5 minutes. Transfer the bacon to a paper towel–lined plate to drain, reserving the fat in the Dutch oven.

2. Add the butter, celery, onion, and garlic and stir to coat. Continue to cook, stirring occasionally, until the onion is translucent, about 8 minutes.

3. Add the flour, pepper, and thyme, stirring until the flour is golden and toasted, about 3 minutes. Stir in the salt, potatoes, clam juice, and chicken stock and bring the soup to a simmer, then cover and cook until the potatoes are fork-tender, about 20 minutes more. Remove from heat and stir in the half-and-half, clams, and cooked bacon.

4. Divide the soup among the bowls. Top with chives, pepper (if desired), and oyster crackers to serve.

TOUCHDOWN TIP: *Transfer the finished soup to a portable slow cooker to keep it toasty warm all day. This recipe is made for a 6-quart vessel (or larger).*

WISCONSIN BOOYAH

One of the defining dishes of the Midwest—and also a favorite '90s insult—booyah is a staple on game day. The originators of this soup might have been Belgian or French immigrants, but now it's all American. A mix of chicken and beef, plus hearty bites of veggies, make for a filling and warming pot of soup. Don't forget the oyster crackers!

======================== SERVES 8 TO 10 ========================

2 tablespoons **extra-virgin olive oil**

1 large **white onion**, chopped

1 pound **boneless, skinless chicken thighs**, cut into 1-inch pieces

1 pound **boneless beef chuck**, cut into 1-inch pieces

1 tablespoon **kosher salt**

1 teaspoon **freshly ground black pepper**

4 cups **chicken** or **beef stock**

1 tablespoon **Worcestershire sauce** or **soy sauce**

1 (28-ounce) can **crushed tomatoes**

1 pound **Russet potatoes**, cut into ½-inch pieces

2 stalks **celery**, thinly sliced

2 cups **shredded cabbage** or **coleslaw mix**

4 cups **frozen mixed vegetables** (green beans, carrots, corn, and/or peas)

Oyster crackers, for serving

1. Heat the oil in a large Dutch oven over medium-high heat. When the oil is shimmering, add the onion and cook for about 5 minutes, stirring frequently, until softened. Add the chicken, beef, salt, and pepper, and stir to combine. Cook for about 5 minutes, stirring occasionally, until the meat starts to brown.

2. Add the stock, Worcestershire sauce, and tomatoes and bring to a simmer. Once simmering, cover, reduce the heat to medium-low, and cook for about 1 hour, until the meat is tender. Transfer the meat to a plate.

3. Increase the heat to medium-high, return to a simmer, and add the potatoes, celery, and cabbage. Cover and cook for about 10 minutes, or until the potatoes are fork-tender. Meanwhile, use two forks to shred the chicken and beef.

4. Return the shredded meat to the Dutch oven, along with the frozen vegetables. Cover and cook for about 5 minutes, until everything is warmed through. Divide the soup among bowls and serve with oyster crackers.

TOUCHDOWN TIP: *Transfer the finished soup to a portable slow cooker to keep it toasty warm all day. This recipe is made for a 6-quart vessel (or larger).*

CHICKEN POT PIE SOUP

As if this creamy mix of chicken, potatoes, peas, and carrots couldn't be more delicious, it gets topped with a piece of puff pastry dough for all the flaky goodness of a classic pot pie. If this bowl doesn't win the day, we don't know what will.

SERVES 8 TO 10

1 sheet **frozen puff pastry dough**

Smoked paprika

2 pounds **boneless, skinless chicken thighs**

2 teaspoons **kosher salt**

1 teaspoon **freshly ground black pepper**

2 tablespoons (¼ stick) **unsalted butter**

1 large **white onion**, finely chopped

2 **garlic cloves**, minced

¼ cup **all-purpose flour**

4 cups **chicken stock**

2 cups **whole milk**

1 pound **Yukon Gold potatoes**, cut into ½-inch pieces

4 cups **frozen peas** and **carrots**

2 tablespoons chopped **fresh parsley**

1. Preheat the oven to 450°F with a rack in the center. Line a rimmed baking sheet with parchment paper.

2. Unroll the puff pastry, then cut it into 8 or 10 strips along the short edge. Arrange them in one even layer on the prepared baking sheet and bake according to the package instructions. Remove from the oven, sprinkle with paprika, and let cool.

3. Meanwhile, season the chicken with 1 teaspoon of the salt and ½ teaspoon of the pepper. Melt the butter in a large Dutch oven over medium-high heat. Add the chicken and cook until browned on the outside and cooked through, about 6 minutes per side. Transfer the chicken to a plate.

4. Add the onion to the Dutch oven and cook for about 5 minutes, stirring frequently, until softened. Add the garlic and cook until fragrant, about 1 minute more. Add the flour and cook, whisking constantly, for about 2 minutes, or until the flour is golden brown and fragrant. Add the chicken stock, milk, and the remaining 1 teaspoon salt and ½ teaspoon pepper and bring to a simmer. Add the potatoes, then cover, and cook until the potatoes are fork-tender, about 20 minutes more.

5. Use two forks to shred the chicken, then return it to the Dutch oven and add the frozen peas and carrots and parsley. Simmer for about 2 minutes, or until the chicken and vegetables are warmed through.

6. Divide the soup among bowls and top each with a piece of pastry to serve.

TOUCHDOWN TIP: *Cool the pastry and store it in an airtight container. Transfer the finished soup to a portable slow cooker to keep it toasty warm all day. This recipe is made for a 6-quart vessel (or larger).*

NO STRESS
MAKE-AHEAD RIBS

Ribs are always a good idea. But manning a low-and-slow grill for hours on end? Not the vibe. This recipe leaves all the precooking to the oven, for ribs that are perfectly tender with no stress. All you have to do on game day is slather them in sauce, get them hot and sticky on the grill, and keep your lips zipped when anyone asks for the recipe.

=== SERVES 8 ===

1 tablespoon **kosher salt**

1 tablespoon **garlic powder**

1 tablespoon **onion powder**

1 tablespoon **ground cumin**

1 tablespoon **chili powder**

1 tablespoon **smoked paprika**

2 teaspoons **freshly ground black pepper**

2 racks **baby back ribs**

2 cups **barbecue sauce**, store-bought or homemade *(see page 118)* plus more for serving

1. Preheat the oven to 300°F with a rack in the center. Line a rimmed baking sheet with foil.

2. In a small bowl, whisk the salt, garlic powder, onion powder, cumin, chili powder, paprika, and pepper to combine. Place the ribs on the prepared baking sheet and blanket both sides with the seasoning mix. Cover the baking sheet tightly with foil and transfer to the oven. Bake the ribs until the meat is tender, about 2 hours.

3. Transfer the ribs to a cutting board and let cool completely, about 1 hour.

4. When ready to serve, prep a grill for high heat *(see page 17)*.

5. Slather the ribs on both sides with the barbecue sauce. Place them bone-side down on the grill and cook, covered, for about 5 minutes, until the sauce is sticky and the ribs are warmed through. Slice the ribs and serve immediately with extra barbecue sauce.

TOUCHDOWN TIP: *If you don't have access to a grill, preheat the oven to 500°F. Brush the ribs with the barbecue sauce and bake on the foil-lined baking sheet, uncovered, for 10 minutes.*

LOADED HOT DOG BAR

There are people who open a couple packs of franks, leave squishy buns in the bag, and set out a half-empty ketchup bottle. Then there are serious players who know the rules for a valid hot dog bar. If you want to up your dog game, follow this simple philosophy:

FEEDS A CROWD

RULE 1: Pick a variety of wieners. Hot dogs are excellent, but so are sausages and brats in all flavors. Be nice to your friends and grab one vegan option, too.

RULE 2: Buns should always be toasted. Potato buns are the standard move, but mini rolls and pretzel buns add some variety. And again: Always. Toasted.

RULE 3: The toppings should be a mix of spicy, savory, sweet, acidic, creamy, and crunchy. The dog and bun are merely a vessel for your culinary best.

RULE 4: Make two hot dogs per person. Even if they "only want one," they're probably going back for seconds.

Vegetable oil, for the grill

Hot dogs, sausages, bratwursts, or vegan dogs

Buns in any style

Condiments and **toppings**

1. Preheat the grill for two heat zones: high direct heat and indirect heat *(see page 17)*.

2. Grill the hot dogs and/or vegan dogs over direct heat, uncovered, for 2 to 3 minutes per side, or until the outside has a nice char and they are warmed through.

3. Sausages and brats should be placed over indirect heat, covered, and cooked for 15 to 20 minutes, flipping halfway, until cooked through. Transfer to direct heat and cook uncovered for a quick char, about 2 minutes per side.

4. Buns can be placed on the upper rack or over indirect heat to slowly toast.

5. Arrange platters of cooked dogs and toasted buns alongside condiments and toppings, and allow everyone to make their own dream dog.

CONDIMENTS

Sriracha	Ketchup	Ranch dressing
Relish	Queso	Buffalo sauce
Mustard	Mayonnaise	BBQ sauce

TOPPINGS

Kimchi	Sliced scallions	Shredded cheese
Crumbled cooked bacon	Shredded lettuce	Sautéed peppers and onions
Sliced pickled jalapeños	Diced onion	Diced pineapple
	Crushed chips	Refried beans
	Tomato slices	

If your guests need some inspiration, here are some of our favorite flavor combos:

Hawaiian Dog

Ketchup, crumbled bacon, shredded cheese, diced pineapple, pickled jalapeños

Nacho Dog

Queso, refried beans, pickled jalapeños, diced onion, crushed chips

BLT Dog

Mayo, tomato slices, shredded lettuce, crumbled bacon

Korean BBQ Dog

BBQ sauce, sriracha, kimchi, sliced scallions, shredded lettuce

Buffalo Dog

Buffalo sauce, ranch dressing, shredded cheese, diced onion, crumbled bacon

Hawaiian Dog

Korean BBQ Dog

BLT Dog

Nacho Dog

Buffalo Dog

BBQ PORK NACHOS

Nachos are a stadium staple. But we're going big and bold with shredded BBQ pork, a bean-and-cheese sauce, and all the right toppings. For best results, make them a day ahead so the pork can soak up all those delicious flavors! These are nacho mama's nachos.

======= FEEDS A CROWD =======

PORK:

2 pounds **boneless pork shoulder**, cut into 2-inch pieces

1 tablespoon **ground cumin**

2 teaspoons **kosher salt**

1 teaspoon **freshly ground black pepper**

1 cup **barbecue sauce**, store-bought or homemade *(see page 118)*

1 cup **lager beer**

4 **garlic cloves**, smashed

BEAN SAUCE:

1 (16-ounce) can **refried beans**

1 cup **spicy salsa**

1 cup **sour cream**

16 slices **American cheese**

NACHOS:

1 (18-ounce) bag **tortilla chips**

2 cups **shredded pepper jack cheese**

FOR SERVING:

Sliced or diced **avocado**

Sliced **pickled jalapeños**

Thinly sliced **scallions**

Sour cream

1. **PREPARE THE PORK:** Season the pork with the cumin, salt, and black pepper. Add the pork, barbecue sauce, beer, and garlic to a large Dutch oven and bring to a simmer over medium-high heat. Cover, reduce the heat to low, and cook for about 2 hours, until the pork is tender and shreds easily.

   Remove the pot from the heat, use tongs to shred the pork in the Dutch oven, and toss to coat in the sauce. Cover to keep warm.

2. **MAKE THE BEAN SAUCE:** Add the refried beans, salsa, sour cream, and cheese to a medium saucepan over low heat. Cook, stirring occasionally, until everything has melted into a coheseive sauce, about 5 minutes. Cover to keep warm and remove from the heat.

3. Preheat the oven to 400°F with a rack in the center. Line a rimmed baking sheet with foil.

4. **ASSEMBLE THE NACHOS:** Spread the chips out on the prepared baking sheet and sprinkle them with cheese. Transfer to the oven and bake for about 5 minutes, or until the cheese starts to melt. Using tongs, distribute the pulled pork evenly over the nachos, then drizzle with the cheese sauce. Return to the oven and bake for about 5 minutes more, or until the nachos are sizzling. Top with avocado, jalapeños, scallions, and sour cream to serve.

TOUCHDOWN TIP: *To prepare these on the grill, bring all the elements premade. Load the chips, cheese, pork, and sauce on the baking sheet and cook on a hot grill for about 5 minutes, or until warm and melty.*

SPICY BEER CAN CHICKEN

Here's the thing with beer can chicken: it might seem like a redneck specialty, but it's actually the smartest invention since . . . well, beer in a can. While the skin gets brown and crispy, the steam from the beer keeps the meat insanely moist, from the breast all the way down to the drumsticks. Plus a sweet-and-spicy rub keeps every juicy bite loaded with flavor. There's no reason not to make this a go-to.

=== SERVES 6 ===

2 tablespoons (packed) **light brown sugar**

1 tablespoon **kosher salt**

1 tablespoon **freshly ground black pepper**

1 tablespoon **onion powder**

1 tablespoon **garlic powder**

1 tablespoon **smoked paprika**

1 tablespoon **chili powder**

1 tablespoon **cayenne pepper**

4 tablespoons (½ stick) **unsalted butter**, melted

1 (5-pound) **whole chicken**, rinsed and patted dry

Vegetable oil, for the grill

1 (16-ounce) can **lager beer**

1. In a medium bowl, whisk the brown sugar, salt, black pepper, onion powder, garlic powder, paprika, chili powder, and cayenne to combine.

2. Rub the melted butter all over the chicken. Sprinkle 3 tablespoons of the spice mixture in the cavity of the chicken, then rub the rest of the spice mixture all over the outside, getting under the breast skin and coating the legs and wings thoroughly.

3. Prep the grill for medium direct/indirect heat *(see page 17)* and oil the grates.

4. Pour about half of the beer into a glass, then insert the can with the remaining beer into the chicken's cavity. Place the chicken and can, sitting upright, in a skillet on the indirect side of the grill. Cover and cook for about 1 hour 30 minutes, until a meat thermometer inserted into the thickest part of the chicken thigh reads 165°F. (Keep an eye on the grill temperature to make sure it's always hovering between 325°F and 350°F.)

   If you're preparing the chicken in the oven, preheat to 350°F with a rack in the lower third. Place the chicken and can, sitting upright, in a 9 × 13-inch baking dish, then transfer it to the oven. Bake for about 1 hour 30 minutes, until a meat thermometer inserted into the thickest part of the chicken thigh reads 165°F.

5. Use tongs to remove the beer can and transfer the chicken to a cutting board. Let the chicken rest for 15 to 20 minutes before carving.

TOUCHDOWN TIP: *For unbelievable flavor, coat the chicken in the spice rub, then place it on a rimmed baking sheet, breast-side up and uncovered, and refrigerate for up to 24 hours. Bring to room temp before grilling.*

SLOPPY JOE SUB

If you're trying to decide what to feed a crowd, here's a no-brainer. Sloppy joes take two seconds to make (okay, 15 minutes, but still). Everything gets piled on a sub, covered with cheese, and baked until warm and gooey. It's a guaranteed touchdown.

SERVES 8

4 strips **thick-cut bacon**, cut into small pieces

1 **red bell pepper**, diced

1 **white onion**, diced

1 pound **ground beef**

1 cup **ketchup**

2 tablespoons (packed) **light brown sugar**

1 tablespoon **Worcestershire sauce**

1 tablespoon **Dijon mustard**

1 tablespoon **smoked paprika**

1 teaspoon **chili powder**

½ teaspoon **kosher salt**

1 large **Italian loaf**, halved lengthwise

8 slices **American cheese**

1. Preheat the oven to 350°F with a rack in the lower third.

2. Add the bacon to a large skillet. Cook over medium heat for about 5 minutes, stirring occasionally, or until the fat starts to render. Add the bell pepper and onion, and cook, stirring occasionally, until the onion has started to soften, about 5 minutes more.

3. Add the ground beef, ketchup, brown sugar, Worcestershire sauce, mustard, paprika, chili powder, and salt, breaking the beef up with a wooden spoon, and cook about 10 minutes, or until the meat is tender and the sauce has thickened.

4. Stack two large pieces of foil and one piece of parchment paper on a flat work surface. Place the bread halves on the parchment and scoop some of the bread from the center of each half. Pile the sloppy joe mixture into the hollowed-out bottom half. Lay the slices of cheese over the meat, then firmly press the top of the bread down over it. Roll the sandwich tightly in the parchment, then wrap tightly with both layers of foil.

5. Bake for about 10 minutes, or until the bread is warm and the cheese is gooey. Remove from the oven and discard the foil. Keeping the parchment in place, use a serrated knife to cut the sandwich into 8 pieces. Serve immediately.

TOUCHDOWN TIP: *To prepare on the grill, prep the grill for medium direct/indirect heat (see page 17). Set the wrapped sandwich over indirect heat, cover, and cook for 5 minutes, then flip the sandwich over and grill 5 minutes more. Discard the foil, slice, and serve.*

CLASSIC
BARBECUE CHICKEN

Is a cookout really a cookout if it doesn't have barbecue chicken? Not to us! This recipe will ensure juicy, tender, and perfectly charred chicken every time. And, hey, no shame in grabbing a bottle of your favorite sauce, but if there was ever a time to show off with homemade BBQ sauce, this is it. Our quick and easy recipe, loaded with flavor and just the right amount of heat, will nail it every time.

SERVES 8

2 pounds **bone-in, skin-on chicken thighs**

2 pounds **drumsticks**

1 tablespoon **kosher salt**

1 tablespoon **light brown sugar**

1 teaspoon **smoked paprika**

1 teaspoon **chili powder**

1 teaspoon **garlic powder**

½ teaspoon **freshly ground black pepper**

Vegetable oil, for the grill

Barbecue Sauce, homemade (recipe follows) or store-bought

1. In a large bowl, add the chicken thighs, drumsticks, salt, brown sugar, paprika, chili powder, garlic powder, and pepper and toss to coat. Cover the bowl with plastic wrap and refrigerate for at least 4 hours.

2. Let the chicken come to room temperature.

3. Prep the grill for medium direct/indirect heat (see page 17) and oil the grates.

4. Arrange the chicken over direct heat and grill, uncovered, for about 4 minutes, flipping halfway, until browned. Transfer the chicken to indirect heat and cook, covered, for about 20 minutes, flipping every 5 minutes. Grill, flipping and generously brushing the chicken with barbecue sauce, 10 to 15 minutes more, or until a meat thermometer inserted into the thickest part of the chicken thigh reads 165°F.

5. Remove the chicken from the grill, cover with foil, and let rest for 10 minutes before serving.

TOUCHDOWN TIP: *Coating chicken in a spice rub and leaving it in the fridge is called dry brining. The longer you can brine, the more you're guaranteed juicy, tender, and thoroughly seasoned chicken. We recommend 4 hours minimum, but 24 is the real move.*

Recipe Continues

Barbecue Sauce

1 tablespoon **vegetable oil**

1 medium **white onion**, halved and thinly sliced

4 **garlic cloves**, smashed

¼ cup (packed) **light brown sugar**

2 tablespoons **smoked paprika**

1 tablespoon **chili powder**

1 teaspoon **cayenne pepper**

1 cup **ketchup**

2 tablespoons **Worcestershire sauce**

2 tablespoons **apple cider vinegar**

2 tablespoons **molasses**

1 tablespoon **Dijon mustard**

½ teaspoon **kosher salt**

Heat the oil in a medium saucepan over medium heat. When the oil is shimmering, add the onion and cook for about 5 minutes, stirring occasionally, until it has started to soften. Stir in the garlic, brown sugar, paprika, chili powder, cayenne, and ¼ cup water. Cook for about 2 minutes, or until the spices are fragrant and the water has evaporated.

Stir in the ketchup, Worcestershire sauce, vinegar, molasses, mustard, and salt. When the sauce starts to bubble, reduce the heat to low and cook, stirring constantly, until the sauce is thick and glossy, about 5 minutes. Let cool for about 10 minutes, then transfer to a blender and blend on high until smooth. Store in an airtight container in the refrigerator for up to 1 week.

GRILLED
ITALIAN HOAGIE

Everything that's great about an Italian sub—the soft bread, the meats, the dressing—is all here, but in the warmest and toastiest form imaginable. A truly stacked sandwich gets rolled up and quickly grilled until the cheese is oozing and the oil-and-vin is dripping down the sides. This is one sandwich guaranteed to disappear in a flash.

SERVES 8

2 packed cups **arugula**

1 (4-ounce) jar **pimientos**, drained and finely chopped

½ medium **red onion**, thinly sliced

¼ cup **red wine vinegar**

2 tablespoons **extra-virgin olive oil**

1 teaspoon **kosher salt**

1 teaspoon **freshly ground black pepper**

1 teaspoon **dried oregano**

1 teaspoon **dried parsley**

1 teaspoon **dried basil**

1 large **Italian loaf**, halved lengthwise

4 tablespoons **mayonnaise**

4 ounces sliced **provolone**

4 ounces sliced **hard salami**

4 ounces sliced **sandwich pepperoni**

4 ounces sliced **mortadella**

1. Prep the grill for medium direct/indirect heat *(see page 17)*.

2. Add the arugula, pimientos, onion, vinegar, olive oil, salt, pepper, oregano, parsley, and basil to a medium bowl and toss to coat. Let marinate for at least 10 minutes.

3. Stack two large pieces of foil and one piece of parchment paper on a flat work surface. Place the bread on the parchment and spread 2 tablespoons of the mayonnaise on each half. Stack the provolone, salami, pepperoni, and mortadella on the bottom half. Add the dressed arugula on top, then firmly press the top of the bread down over the bottom. Roll the sandwich tightly in the parchment, then wrap with both layers of foil.

4. Place the sandwich on the grill over indirect heat, cover, and cook for 5 minutes, then flip the sandwich over and grill 5 minutes more. (You may have to gently press the sandwich onto the grates to get it to stay put.)

5. Remove and discard the foil. Keeping the parchment in place, use a serrated knife to cut the sandwich into 8 pieces. Serve immediately.

TOUCHDOWN TIP: *To prepare in the oven, bake the wrapped sandwich at 350°F for about 10 minutes until warm and gooey. Discard the foil and slice as above.*

COLA BURGERS

A mixture of soda and French dressing seems weird on paper, but just trust us. You're about to experience a burger that's juicy AF and unbelievably seasoned. The soda gives great texture, unexpected flavor, and tons of moisture. French dressing adds an enormous savory punch that makes the burger taste more burger-y. And brushing the glaze over top gives a perfectly caramelized char to the outside, making every bite taste like it's fresh off the grill. We'll never catch you flipping plain patties again.

SERVES 8

Vegetable oil, for the grill

1 **large egg**

¾ cup **cola**

¾ cup **French salad dressing**

1 teaspoon **kosher salt**

½ teaspoon **freshly ground black pepper**

25 crushed **saltines** (about 1 cup)

2 pounds **ground beef**

FOR SERVING:

Hamburger buns

Lettuce

Sliced **tomato**

Sliced **red onion**

Pickle chips

1. Prep the grill for medium heat *(see page 17)* and oil the grates.

2. In a large bowl, whisk the egg, ½ cup of the cola, ½ cup of the French dressing, the salt, and pepper to combine. Crumble the crushed crackers and ground beef into the bowl, then use your hands to combine. Divide the meat into 8 equal portions and pat them into 1-inch-thick patties.

3. In a small bowl, whisk the remaining ¼ cup each cola and French dressing to combine. Brush the tops of the patties with the cola mixture, then place the patties cola-side down on the grill. Cover and cook for about 3 minutes, or until nicely charred. Brush the top side with the cola mixture, then flip and cook for about 3 minutes more. Continue brushing and flipping until the burgers have reached their desired doneness.

4. While the burgers grill, split the buns and arrange them on the top rack to toast. Top the buns with the grilled burgers and serve the desired toppings on the side.

TOUCHDOWN TIP: *A meat thermometer will help nail burgers every time. Medium-rare is 130°F, medium is 140°F, medium-well is 150°F, and well-done is 160°F.*

SAUSAGE and ONION
STUFFED PEPPERS

The dream team of sausage, onion, and peppers has already conquered pastas, pizzas, and subs. So, what's left at this late stage in their career? An all-in-one play, of course. The pepper gets stuffed with sausage and onion (and some bubbly melted cheese on top because obviously). It's these kinds of innovative plays that will make you the Tailgate MVP.

SERVES 4

4 medium **bell peppers**

1 teaspoon **kosher salt**

½ teaspoon **freshly ground black pepper**

1 tablespoon **extra-virgin olive oil**

1 pound **sweet or spicy Italian sausage**, casings removed

1 medium **red onion**, halved and thinly sliced

2 **garlic cloves**, minced

1 teaspoon **ground cumin**

1 teaspoon **dried oregano**

½ teaspoon **fennel seeds**

8 slices **provolone cheese**

1. Preheat the oven to 400°F with a rack in the center.

2. Slice off the tops of the bell peppers and scoop out the seeds and ribs. Place the peppers in an 8 × 8-inch baking dish. Season the insides of the peppers with the salt and pepper.

3. Heat the oil in a large skillet over medium-high heat. When the oil is shimmering, add the sausage and cook for about 5 minutes, breaking it apart with a wooden spoon, until no pink remains. Add the onion, garlic, cumin, oregano, and fennel, and cook, stirring occasionally, for about 5 minutes more, or until the onions have started to soften.

4. Fill each pepper to the top with the sausage filling. Pour 1 cup water into the bottom of the baking dish. Tightly cover the dish with foil and transfer it to the oven. Bake for about 30 minutes, or until the water has evaporated and the peppers are tender. Uncover and place 2 slices of the provolone on each pepper. Bake until the cheese has melted and is starting to brown, about 10 minutes more. Serve immediately.

TOUCHDOWN TIP: *To make this on the grill, prepare the filling, stuff the peppers, and pack in an aluminum baking pan ahead of time. Prep the grill for medium direct/indirect heat (see page 17), place the baking pan over indirect heat, and cover. Grill for 20 to 30 minutes, until the water evaporates. Remove the foil and cover the grill for about 5 minutes, until the cheese is melted.*

CHICKEN PARM PIZZA

What could be better than eating the two best things? Answer: Eating them both in the exact same bite. A huge, circular, breaded chicken parm becomes the base for a warm and cheesy pizza, blanketed in marinara and gooey pools of mozz. It's probably not compatible with any kind of diet, but game day is no time for excuses. Get in there and go hard!

SERVES 8

Nonstick cooking spray

1 pound **ground chicken**

2 cups **breadcrumbs**

1 teaspoon **kosher salt**

1 teaspoon **freshly ground black pepper**

1 teaspoon **dried oregano**

1 teaspoon **garlic powder**

1 teaspoon **onion powder**

1 cup **marinara sauce**

1 (8-ounce) bag **shredded mozzarella cheese**

¼ cup grated **Parmesan cheese**

Whole fresh basil, for serving

1. Preheat the oven to 400°F with a rack in the center. Line a rimmed baking sheet with foil and coat with nonstick spray.

2. Add the chicken, breadcrumbs, salt, pepper, oregano, garlic powder, and onion powder to a large bowl and use your hands to combine. Transfer the chicken mixture to the prepared baking sheet and pat it into a 10-inch round circle, about ½ inch thick. Bake for about 20 minutes, or until the center of the circle is cooked through and golden brown. Remove from the oven and increase the oven temperature to 500°F.

3. Spoon the marinara sauce over the surface of the chicken, leaving a 1-inch border for crust. Sprinkle the mozzarella and Parmesan on top and bake for about 5 minutes, or until the cheese has melted and is starting to brown.

4. Top the pizza with basil to serve.

MEXICAN CORN SALAD

All the joy of biting into elote (for the uninitiated, that's grilled corn slathered in mayo and chili powder) without the messy chaos of corn on the cob! This side is loaded with the charred goodness of grilled corn, a zesty zing from the lime and scallions, fresh cilantro, salty cotija, and a little kick of chili powder. It's so quick to throw together and gone almost as fast!

SERVES 8

2 tablespoons **vegetable oil**

1 (12-ounce) bag **frozen corn**, thawed

½ teaspoon **kosher salt**

¼ teaspoon **freshly ground black pepper**

4 **scallions**, thinly sliced

¼ cup chopped **fresh cilantro**, leaves and tender stems

½ cup **cotija cheese**, plus more for serving

Juice of 1 **lime**

2 tablespoons **mayonnaise**

2 tablespoons **chili powder**, plus more for serving

1. Heat the oil in a large nonstick skillet over medium-high heat. When the oil is shimmering, add the corn, salt, and pepper. Stir to coat, then arrange the corn in an even layer and cook undisturbed for about 4 minutes, or until the bottom is charred. Toss and continue to cook, stirring occasionally, until the corn is tender, about 2 minutes more. Transfer to a large bowl.

2. Add the scallions, cilantro, cotija, lime juice, mayonnaise, and chili powder to the bowl and toss to coat. Let the corn mixture cool for about 15 minutes, then cover it tightly with plastic wrap and refrigerate for at least 2 hours and up to 12 hours.

3. Top with more cotija and chili powder before serving.

CORNBREAD SALAD

When you have a big crowd to feed, this salad (and we're really stretching the limits of that word here) is a guaranteed path to victory. Not only is it big and beautiful, it's also loaded with everything under the sun: veggies, beans, cheese, bacon, ranch, and, as the title suggests, even cornbread. It's a cheap and delicious way to amp up any meal.

SERVES 10 TO 12

1 (8.5-ounce) box **cornbread mix**, plus additional ingredients according to box instructions

1 cup **sour cream**

1 cup **mayonnaise**

1 (1-ounce) packet **ranch seasoning**

1 (28-ounce) can **diced tomatoes**, drained

1 **red bell pepper**, diced

1 **green bell pepper**, diced

1 (29-ounce) can **pinto beans**, rinsed and drained

1 (12-ounce) bag **frozen corn**, thawed

1 (8-ounce) bag **shredded cheddar cheese**

10 strips **thick-cut bacon**, cooked and crumbled

4 **scallions**, thinly sliced

1. Bake the cornbread according to package directions. Cool completely in the pan, about 30 minutes.

2. While the cornbread cools, combine the sour cream, mayonnaise, and ranch seasoning in a small bowl. In a medium bowl, combine the tomatoes and red and green bell peppers.

3. In a 4-quart glass bowl, crumble half of the cornbread. Top with half of the beans, half of the tomato mixture, half of the corn, half of the ranch mixture, half of the cheese, and half of the bacon. Repeat with the remaining ingredients.

4. Garnish with the scallions. Cover tightly with plastic wrap and refrigerate for at least 2 hours and up to 12 hours before serving.

TOUCHDOWN TIP: *A regular glass bowl works fine, but a trifle bowl puts this showstopper on a pedestal.*

REFRESHING
WATERMELON SALAD

This salad is perfect for holding on to the last days of summer. Tangy lime, spicy jalapeño, savory onion, herby basil, spicy chili powder, and salty cheese—the gang's all here. Sliced watermelon is great on its own, but when playing with this team, it reaches new heights.

SERVES 10 TO 12

Zest and juice of 2 **limes**

1 medium **red onion**, halved and thinly sliced

2 **jalapeños**, seeded (optional) and diced

1 cup torn **fresh basil leaves**

1 (10-pound) **watermelon**, cubed (about 16 cups)

2 tablespoons **chili powder**, plus more for serving

¼ cup crumbled **cotija** or **feta cheese**, plus more for serving

1. In a large bowl, combine the lime zest and juice, onion, jalapeños, and basil. Add the watermelon, chili powder, and cotija, and toss to coat. Cover and refrigerate for at least 1 hour and up to overnight.

2. Sprinkle with more cotija and chili powder to serve.

TRICOLOR PASTA SALAD

Here are the two key plays when making pasta salad: undercook and overdress. Cooking the pasta to slightly *under* al dente seems like it might make for a tough sell. But here comes part two: when the pasta absorbs all that delicious *extra* dressing, it turns soft and plump without getting mushy. Stick to this golden rule and you'll nail it every time.

SERVES 8

1 (12-ounce) box **tricolor rotini pasta**

½ cup **extra-virgin olive oil**

¼ cup **red wine vinegar**

¼ cup grated **Parmesan cheese**

2 **garlic cloves**, grated

1 tablespoon **dried basil**

1 tablespoon **dried oregano**

1 teaspoon **kosher salt**

½ teaspoon **freshly ground black pepper**

1 **green bell pepper**, diced

1 **red bell pepper**, diced

1 medium **red onion**, halved and thinly sliced

½ cup roughly chopped **fresh parsley**

4 ounces sliced **hard salami**, julienned

4 ounces **provolone cheese**, cubed

1 (12-ounce) can sliced **ripe olives**, drained

1. Bring a large pot of water to a boil over high heat. Cook the pasta for 1 minute less than specified in the package directions.

2. Meanwhile, place the olive oil, vinegar, Parmesan, garlic, basil, oregano, salt, and pepper in a large bowl, and whisk to combine. Drain the pasta and immediately add it to the bowl. Toss to coat.

3. Add the green and red bell peppers, onion, parsley, salami, provolone, and olives to the bowl and toss to combine. Let the pasta mixture cool for about 30 minutes before covering the bowl with plastic wrap. Refrigerate until ready to serve.

TOUCHDOWN TIP: *The pasta absorbs more flavor the longer it sits. Make it the day before and chill overnight.*

BAKED BEANS

We're not necessarily trying to break the rules of a classic pot of Boston baked beans; we're just taking the opportunity to improve on a fan favorite. Root beer is the ultimate shortcut to a sweet and deeply spiced pot of beans, and using canned beans is an even greater shortcut that avoids a long day of simmering. It seems like it wouldn't matter, but investing in a *really* good root beer makes all the difference. Sioux City, Virgil's, and even a hard root beer, like Not Your Father's, are all good options.

SERVES 8

4 strips **thick-cut bacon**, cut into small pieces

1 large **yellow onion**, diced

2 **garlic cloves**, minced

2 (29-ounce) cans **cannellini beans**, drained and rinsed

1 (12-ounce) can **root beer**

2 tablespoons **yellow mustard**

2 tablespoons **tomato paste**

2 tablespoons **light molasses**

2 tablespoons **apple cider vinegar**

2 teaspoons **chili powder**

1 teaspoon **kosher salt**

1 teaspoon **freshly ground black pepper**

1. Add the bacon to a large Dutch oven or saucepan. Cook the bacon over medium heat, stirring occasionally, until most of the fat has rendered, about 4 minutes. Add the onion and cook until translucent, about 6 minutes. Stir in the garlic and cook until very fragrant, about 1 minute more.

2. Add the beans, root beer, mustard, tomato paste, molasses, vinegar, chili powder, salt, and pepper and stir to combine. Bring to a simmer, then cover and cook for 20 to 30 minutes, until the sauce has thickened; simmer uncovered for 5 minutes more if the sauce isn't quite thick enough. Serve immediately.

BLISTERED
SHISHITO PEPPERS

Shishito peppers are the Russian roulette of side dishes. Nine out of ten are mild with an earthy pepper flavor, just watch out for the one with the attitude. But the momentary spice hit is all part of the fun, and it doesn't linger. Plus, a sip of a beer cocktail *(see page 173)* will cool things down even faster. Smoked paprika adds some savory seasoning, while sesame seeds and flaky sea salt give an excellent crunch factor. Because the skillet needs to be screaming hot, this is an ideal dish to make on the grill, where the smoke and savory smells will attract attention from all over the parking lot.

===== SERVES 8 =====

1 tablespoon **vegetable oil**

1 pound **shishito peppers**

1 teaspoon **kosher salt**

2 tablespoons **sesame seeds**

1 tablespoon **smoked paprika**

Flaky sea salt, for serving

1. Heat a large cast-iron skillet over high heat for about 5 minutes. When hot, add the vegetable oil and swirl to coat the skillet, then immediately add the peppers, shaking to even them out. Sear on one side, undisturbed for 3 minutes, until charred in spots. Add the kosher salt and toss the skillet to season and redistribute the peppers. Sear for about 2 minutes more, or until the peppers are starting to soften. Remove from the heat and immediately add the sesame seeds and paprika, then toss to coat.

2. Sprinkle with flaky sea salt and serve immediately.

MEDITERRANEAN SALAD
with HUMMUS DRESSING

Until now, Mediterranean salads have probably consisted of some ho-hum oil and vinegar dressing that you could take or leave. Enter the absolute joy of hummus dressing. Creamy, tangy, and perfect for all the fresh produce piled up in the bowl, it's the dream team of the season!

SERVES 8

1 **English cucumber**, halved and cut into ½-inch pieces

1 pint **grape tomatoes**, halved

1 medium **red onion**, cut into ½-inch pieces

½ cup roughly chopped **fresh parsley**

1 (10-ounce) jar pitted **kalamata olives**, drained and roughly chopped

1 (6-ounce) package **crumbled feta cheese**

2 cups lightly crushed **baked pita chips**

1 (10-ounce) package **plain hummus**

Juice of 2 **lemons**

½ teaspoon **kosher salt**, plus more as needed

½ teaspoon **freshly ground black pepper**, plus more as needed

1. In a large bowl, combine the cucumber, tomatoes, onion, parsley, olives, feta, and pita chips.

2. Add the hummus, lemon juice, salt, pepper, and 2 tablespoons water to a blender or food processor and blend on high for about 30 seconds, or until a slightly loose dressing forms. Taste and add salt and pepper as needed.

3. Add the dressing to the salad and toss to coat. Serve immediately or cover and refrigerate until ready to serve.

HONEY MUSTARD
BRUSSELS SLAW

Tailgates are great excuse to go wild, but listen, sometimes you need a little green on your plate. Here's a healthy-but-not-boring side that is so delicious it might even be the star player. A mix of shredded Brussels sprouts and red cabbage adds an excellent texture, pecans offer some crunch, the fruit keeps it sweet, Gouda brings the smoke, and the perfect honey mustard dressing wraps it all up. Slaw has never been more delicious!

SERVES 8

SLAW:

1 pound **Brussels sprouts**, trimmed and shredded

1 (10-ounce) bag **shredded red cabbage**

½ cup roughly chopped **toasted pecans**

½ cup **dried cranberries**

½ cup **golden raisins**

4 ounces **smoked Gouda cheese**

DRESSING:

½ cup **extra-virgin olive oil**

¼ cup **apple cider vinegar**

¼ cup **honey**

¼ cup **Dijon mustard**

1 **garlic clove**, grated

½ teaspoon **kosher salt**

1. **MAKE THE SLAW:** In a large bowl, combine the Brussels sprouts, cabbage, pecans, cranberries, and raisins. Use a vegetable peeler or box grater to peel long shreds of the Gouda into the bowl.

2. **MAKE THE DRESSING:** In a small bowl, whisk the olive oil, vinegar, honey, mustard, garlic, and salt until emulsified. Pour the dressing over the slaw and use your hands to massage the dressing into the Brussels sprouts and cabbage.

3. Cover the bowl tightly with plastic wrap and refrigerate for at least 2 hours and up to overnight. Toss again before serving.

SESAME GLAZED
GRILLED VEGGIES

This is a very adult way to eat your veggies. A sweet and sticky sesame glaze is the perfect pairing for smoky grilled veggies, giving them just enough excitement to make this side feel like a team player. Deep char marks and a beautiful brush of glaze only need a quick sprinkle of sesame seeds to be camera-ready.

SERVES 8

Vegetable oil, for the grill

GLAZE:

¼ cup **honey**

2 tablespoons **sesame seeds**, plus more for serving

2 tablespoons **soy sauce**

1 tablespoon **rice vinegar**

2 **garlic cloves**, grated

VEGGIES:

Sesame oil

Kosher salt

2 **baby eggplants** or **Japanese eggplants**, cut lengthwise into ½-inch-thick slices

2 **zucchini**, cut lengthwise into ½-inch-thick slices

2 **yellow squash**, cut lengthwise into ½-inch-thick slices

4 **red bell peppers**, thinly sliced

1. Prep the grill for high heat *(see page 17)* and oil the grates. Alternatively, heat a grill pan over high heat.

2. **MAKE THE GLAZE:** In a medium bowl, whisk the honey, sesame seeds, soy sauce, vinegar, and garlic until well combined.

3. **PREPARE THE VEGGIES:** Brush one side of the vegetable slices with a generous amount of sesame oil and season well with salt. Lay the vegetable slices seasoned-side down on the grill, and cook uncovered for about 4 minutes, until deeply charred. Brush the top side generously with sesame oil and season with salt, then flip and grill them for about 4 minutes more, or until the vegetables are tender. Brush with the glaze, then transfer the veggies, glazed-side down, to a serving platter and brush with the remaining glaze.

4. Sprinkle with sesame seeds and serve immediately.

TOUCHDOWN TIP: *Make sure the grill and the veggies are thoroughly brushed with oil for maximum char with minimal sticking.*

CHOPPED
CHICKEN CAESAR SALAD

Does salad get better than a good chicken Caesar? We could debate that for days, but let's just agree that it's top tier. And really, why mess with perfection? Everything you already love is here—seared chicken, savory dressing, crisp romaine, crunchy croutons, and a generous amount of parm—in an easy-to-eat chopped salad. It's a guaranteed win.

SERVES 8

CHICKEN:

1 tablespoon **extra-virgin olive oil**

1 pound **boneless, skinless chicken breast,** cut into 1-inch pieces

½ teaspoon **kosher salt**

½ teaspoon **freshly ground black pepper**

DRESSING:

1 cup **mayonnaise**

2 tablespoons **Worcestershire sauce**

2 **garlic cloves**

1 teaspoon **Dijon mustard**

1 teaspoon **freshly ground black pepper**

Juice of 1 **lemon**

SALAD:

3 **romaine hearts**

2 cups **croutons**

5 ounces **shaved Parmesan cheese**

1. **COOK THE CHICKEN:** Add the oil to a medium skillet over medium heat. Season the chicken all over with the salt and pepper. When the oil is shimmering, add the chicken, cover, and cook for 6 to 8 minutes, flipping halfway through the cooking time, until the chicken is cooked through. Transfer the chicken to a cutting board and let rest.

2. **MAKE THE DRESSING:** Add the mayonnaise, Worcestershire sauce, garlic, mustard, pepper, and lemon juice to a blender and blend on high until smooth.

3. **ASSEMBLE THE SALAD:** Chop the chicken into small pieces and add them to a large bowl. Cut the romaine hearts into quarters lengthwise, then slice thinly crosswise, stopping just before the root end. Discard the roots and add the sliced lettuce to the bowl. Drizzle with half the dressing and toss to coat. Add the croutons, Parmesan, and remaining dressing and toss before serving.

TOUCHDOWN TIP: *If you want to up your game, slice the romaine hearts in half, brush them generously with oil, and slap them on the grill for about 5 minutes, or until nicely charred.*

TEAM COLORS CAKE

Nothing says team spirit like an entire cake spelling out . . . well, your team spirit. This is the edible equivalent of a shirtless superfan, painted head to toe, screaming in the stands. Get creative and make your mark! And, yeah, of course you could use boxed cake mix and store-bought frosting, but if there was ever a time to go the extra yard, this is it.

SERVES 12

Nonstick cooking spray

7 **large egg whites**, room temperature

1¼ cups (2½ sticks) **unsalted butter**, room temperature

2½ cups **sugar**

4 cups **all-purpose flour**

½ cup **cornstarch**

2 tablespoons **baking powder**

1 teaspoon **kosher salt**

1½ cups **whole milk**

1 tablespoon **vanilla extract**

3 cups **Buttercream Frosting**, store-bought or homemade (recipe follows)

Food coloring, for decorating

1. Preheat the oven to 350°F with a rack in the center. Coat a 9 × 13-inch baking dish with nonstick spray. Line the bottom with parchment paper and spray again.

2. In a stand mixer fitted with the whisk attachment (or using an electric hand mixer and a large bowl), beat the egg whites on medium until stiff peaks form, about 5 minutes.

3. Add the butter to a large bowl, and, using a hand mixer, beat on medium until creamy, about 2 minutes. Gradually add the sugar and beat until the mixture is light and fluffy, about 3 minutes more.

4. Set a mesh strainer over the butter mixture, then sift the flour, cornstarch, baking powder, and salt through the strainer. Using a rubber spatula, fold the sifted ingredients into the butter mixture until combined. Add the milk and vanilla, and beat on medium until a hydrated batter forms, about 30 seconds.

5. Gently fold one-third of the egg whites into the batter with a rubber spatula, being careful not to deflate the eggs too much. Fold in the remaining egg whites in two batches.

6. Pour the batter into the prepared baking dish and smooth the top with the back of a spatula. Bake for about 25 minutes, or until a toothpick inserted in the center comes out clean. Cool completely in the baking dish before frosting.

7. Turn the cake out onto a cooling rack. Peel off the parchment, then slide the cake back into the baking dish. (This turns the cake upside down, creating a flat, smooth work surface.) Use a ruler and a paring knife to divide the cake into 12 equal squares. Divide the frosting among small

Recipe Continues

bowls and mix each one with 2 to 4 drops of food coloring to create your team colors. (Save one bowl of white frosting.) Use an offset spatula to frost the squares in alternating colors. Add some frosting to a piping bag fitted with a tip and pipe white borders around the squares. Decorate with slogans, team symbols, and/or the school name.

8. Chill the cake until ready to serve.

TOUCHDOWN TIP: *The cake and frosting can be made ahead of time and stored separately in the refrigerator for up to 3 days. Allow both to come to room temp and give the buttercream a whip to revive its fluffiness before frosting.*

Buttercream Frosting

MAKES 3 CUPS

½ cup (1 stick) **unsalted butter**, room temperature

1 tablespoon **vanilla extract**

4½ cups **powdered sugar**, plus more as needed

3 tablespoons **whole milk**, plus more as needed

In a stand mixer fitted with the paddle attachment (or using an electric hand mixer and a large bowl), beat the butter on medium until soft and creamy, about 2 minutes. Add the vanilla and powdered sugar and continue beating until the mixture is well combined. Add the milk, 1 tablespoon at time, and beat until fluffy and spreadable. Add more milk or powdered sugar as needed. Store refrigerated in an airtight container for up to 3 days.

S'MORES BROWNIES

When you're outside and cooking over an open fire, it's usually capped off with a round of s'mores. But since this is tailgating—and grilled s'mores just aren't the same (trust us, we tried)—we decided to go with the next best thing: s'mores brownies. Dense and fudgy brownies from the box are the perfect base to carry all the sweet and gooey s'mores flavors straight to the end zone.

MAKES 12 BROWNIES

1 (18.3-ounce) box **fudgy brownies**, plus additional ingredients according to box instructions

1½ cups **Golden Grahams cereal** or **crumbled graham crackers**

1½ cups **mini marshmallows**

1 (4-ounce) bar **milk chocolate**, roughly chopped

1. Bake the brownies in a 9 × 13-inch baking dish, according to the package directions.

2. When the brownies are done, preheat the broiler to high. Sprinkle the cereal and marshmallows over the entire surface of the brownies, then broil for 30 to 60 seconds, just until the marshmallows are toasted and puffy. Remove from the oven and sprinkle the chocolate over the top. Slice into 12 squares and serve immediately, or let the brownies cool to room temperature before slicing and serving.

TOUCHDOWN TIP: *Use a culinary blowtorch instead of the broiler for perfect toasting on the marshmallows.*

POTATO CHIP COOKIES

For sweet-and-salty fiends, it doesn't get much better. A super-soft sugar cookie dough is the perfect match for the ultimate salty snack: potato chips. For an extra touch of extra-ness, we dip each ball of dough in more chips to give the finished cookies a perfect crunchy texture in every bite.

MAKES 24 COOKIES

2 cups (4 sticks) **unsalted butter**, room temperature

1 cup **sugar**

1 teaspoon **vanilla extract**

¼ teaspoon **kosher salt**

3½ cups **all-purpose flour**

2½ cups roughly crushed **potato chips**

1. Preheat the oven to 350°F with two racks in the center. Line two rimmed baking sheets with parchment paper.

2. Use a handheld electric mixer (or stand mixer) on medium to beat the butter and sugar together until light and fluffy, about 2 minutes. Add the vanilla, salt, and half of the flour and beat until the flour is incorporated. Gently fold in the remaining flour and 2 cups of the potato chips with a rubber spatula until just incorporated and the dough is soft and sticky.

3. Place the remaining chips on a small plate. Scoop the cookie dough in rounded ⅛-cup (2-tablespoon) servings and roll into balls. Dip one side of each ball in the chips, then place them on the prepared baking sheets, chip-side up, spacing the cookies about 2 inches apart.

4. Bake for about 10 minutes, turning the baking sheets halfway, until the edges of the cookies are golden brown. Cool on the baking sheets for about 5 minutes before transferring the cookies to a wire rack to cool completely.

TOUCHDOWN TIP: *Use a sturdier chip, like kettle chips or even Pringles, to help keep a crunchy texture while baking.*

SPICED APPLE BARS

This is the best dessert to celebrate the fall, which also happens to be football season—our favorite time of year. Soft and fluffy, with sweet bits of apple and plenty of warming spices, they're a little bit of heaven in every bite. They're excellent when served warm, but somehow even better the next day when the flavors have really settled in together. Basically, this is a win-win.

MAKES 12 BARS

Nonstick cooking spray

½ cup (1 stick) **unsalted butter**, melted

1 cup **granulated sugar**

1 cup packed **light brown sugar**

2 **large eggs**

1 tablespoon **ground cinnamon**

1 teaspoon **baking powder**

1 teaspoon **baking soda**

1 teaspoon **vanilla extract**

½ teaspoon **kosher salt**

½ teaspoon **ground nutmeg**

¼ teaspoon **ground cloves**

¼ teaspoon **ground allspice**

2 cups **all-purpose flour**

½ cup **old-fashioned rolled oats**

1 cup **chopped pecans**

4 **Granny Smith apples**, peeled, cored, and diced

Powdered sugar, for serving

1. Preheat the oven to 350°F with a rack in the center. Coat a 9 × 13-inch baking dish with nonstick spray.

2. Add the butter, granulated sugar, and brown sugar to a large bowl and whisk until combined and a thick paste forms. Add the eggs one at a time, whisking to fully incorporate one before adding the next. Whisk in the cinnamon, baking powder, baking soda, vanilla, salt, nutmeg, cloves, and allspice. Gently fold in the flour, oats, pecans, and apples using a rubber spatula until just incorporated.

3. Pour the batter into the prepared baking dish and bake for 20 to 25 minutes, or until a toothpick inserted in the center comes out clean. Cool in the baking dish for at least 1 hour before slicing. Dust with powdered sugar to serve.

MISSISSIPPI MUD CHEESECAKE

Mississippi Mud Pie is a classic for a reason: it's a deep bench of chocolaty goodness. But with all due respect to Ole Miss, there's a new player in town. A light and fluffy cheesecake layer somehow hits all the right notes and still feels like nothing you've ever had before. It's a guaranteed win every time.

=== SERVES 8 TO 10 ===

Nonstick cooking spray

CRUST:

1 (9-ounce) package **thin chocolate wafer cookies**

½ cup **pecan halves**

3 tablespoons **sugar**

¼ teaspoon **kosher salt**

½ cup (1 stick) **unsalted butter**, melted

FILLING:

4 (8-ounce) packages **cream cheese**, room temperature

1 cup **sugar**

2 tablespoons **all-purpose flour**

1 teaspoon **vanilla extract**

2 **large eggs**, room temperature

1 (12-ounce) bag **semisweet chocolate chips**, melted

TOPPING:

1 (10-ounce) bag **mini marshmallows**

1 (16-ounce) container **chocolate frosting**

⅓ cup **chopped roasted pecans**

1. Preheat the oven to 300°F with a rack in the center. Coat a 9-inch springform pan with nonstick spray.

2. **MAKE THE CRUST:** Add the cookies, pecans, sugar, and salt to a food processor. Process until finely crushed, about 1 minute. Pour in the butter and pulse, scraping down the sides as needed, until combined. Press the crust into the prepared pan, then place it on a rimmed baking sheet and bake for 10 minutes. Remove from the oven and let cool slightly.

3. **MEANWHILE, MAKE THE FILLING:** In a stand mixer fitted with the paddle attachment, beat the cream cheese, sugar, flour, vanilla, and eggs on low until combined. Add the melted chocolate and beat until fully incorporated.

4. Pour the filling into the pan and smooth with a spatula. Bake on the baking sheet for 60 to 75 minutes, or until the edges are set but the center is still wobbly. Turn the oven off and crack open the door slightly. Let the cheesecake cool in the oven for 1 hour, then cover it with plastic wrap and refrigerate for at least 2 hours and up to overnight.

5. Remove the cheesecake from the fridge. Run a butter knife or offset spatula around the edge of the cake. Transfer the cake to a serving plate.

6. **MAKE THE TOPPING:** Add the marshmallows to a medium saucepan and cook on medium heat, stirring occasionally, until the marshmallows melt into a smooth sauce, about 3 minutes. Pour the marshmallow sauce over the top of the cake, letting it drip down the sides. Add the chocolate frosting to the same saucepan and cook, stir occasionally, until the frosting melts into a runny sauce, about 3 minutes. Pour the chocolate over the marshmallow layer, letting it also drip down the sides. Sprinkle the pecans over the top of the cake. Chill the cake until the toppings are set, about 10 minutes.

TOUCHDOWN TIP: *Add the marshmallow and chocolate frosting to piping bags for precise and impressive drips, then fill in the top of the cake with the rest.*

NO-BAKE ECLAIR CAKE

Some people love baking, and some people do not. For those who do, see the rest of this chapter. For those who do not, stay right here. This is the cheap, easy, delicious, and oddly elegant dessert you've been looking for. All you have to do is layer graham crackers and pudding, then pour some melted frosting over top. If you can use a whisk, you're 100 percent qualified!

SERVES 12 TO 15

2 (3.5-ounce) boxes **vanilla pudding mix**

4 cups **whole milk**

1 (16-ounce) box **graham crackers**

2 (16-ounce) containers **chocolate frosting**

1. Add the pudding mix to a large bowl, then slowly pour in the milk while whisking constantly for about 2 minutes, or until the whisk starts to leave streaks in the mixture. Set aside to continue thickening.

2. Place the graham crackers in an even layer on the bottom of a 9 × 13-inch baking dish, breaking crackers as needed to fit. Spoon half of the pudding over the crackers, then smooth the pudding into an even layer. Add another layer of graham crackers, then cover with the remaining pudding. Top with a third layer of graham crackers.

3. Remove the lids and seals from the frosting and microwave the containers on high for about 45 seconds, stirring every 15 seconds, until the frosting is soft and runny. Pour the frosting over the graham crackers, covering the entire surface. Cover the baking dish with plastic wrap and refrigerate for at least 2 hours and up to overnight. Slice into squares and serve.

TOUCHDOWN TIP: *For even coverage on your cake, add half of the pudding to a large zip-top bag. Use scissors to cut a large snip off one corner, then carefully squeeze the pudding over the graham crackers and smooth into an even layer.*

COWBOY COOKIES

There really isn't a wrong choice when it comes to cookies. But Cowboy Cookies are like the ultimate right choice because they're practically every cookie all in one. A soft and sweet cookie dough gets overloaded with oats, pecans, coconut, and, of course, chocolate chips. It's the 10-gallon hat of cookies!

MAKES 24 COOKIES

1½ cups (3 sticks) **unsalted butter**, room temperature

1½ cups **granulated sugar**

1½ cups packed **light brown sugar**

3 **large eggs**

1 tablespoon **baking powder**

1 tablespoon **baking soda**

1 teaspoon **kosher salt**

1 tablespoon **ground cinnamon**

1 tablespoon **vanilla extract**

3 cups **all-purpose flour**

2 cups **old-fashioned rolled oats**

1 (12-ounce) bag **semisweet chocolate chips**

1 (7-ounce) bag **sweetened coconut flakes**

1 (8-ounce) bag **chopped pecans** (about 2 cups)

1. Preheat the oven to 350°F and set two racks in the center of the oven. Line two rimmed baking sheets with parchment paper.

2. In a stand mixer fitted with the paddle attachment, combine the butter, granulated sugar, and brown sugar on medium until light and fluffy, about 2 minutes. Add the eggs one at a time, beating each in completely before adding the next one. Add the baking powder, baking soda, salt, cinnamon, vanilla, and half of the flour and beat again until incorporated. Gently fold in the remaining flour, the oats, chocolate chips, coconut, and pecans using a rubber spatula until a soft and sticky dough forms.

3. Using a ¼-cup measure, portion out the dough and roll it into large balls. Place the dough balls at least 3 inches apart on the prepared baking sheets (about 6 per sheet).

4. Bake for 15 to 20 minutes, turning the baking sheets halfway, until the edges of the cookies are golden brown. Cool on the baking sheets for about 5 minutes before transferring the cookies to a wire rack to cool completely. Let the baking sheets cool completely before baking the remaining dough.

PEANUT BUTTER & JELLY KRISPIES

One of the best parts of childhood was gooey and sticky Rice Krispies treats. The only thing *more* nostalgic than that treat is merging them with another childhood fave: PB&J. The peanut butter—chunky or smooth, pick your side—gets melted down with the marshmallows to blanket the cereal, then the finished bars get a drizzle of sweet jelly to cut the richness. It's maybe the best thing ever.

MAKES 12 SQUARES

Nonstick cooking spray

1 (15-ounce) jar **chunky** or **smooth peanut butter**

1 (10-ounce) bag **mini marshmallows**

6 cups **Rice Krispies cereal**

2 cups **jelly of choice**

1. Coat a 9 × 13-inch baking dish with nonstick spray.

2. Add the peanut butter and marshmallows to a large Dutch oven or saucepan and cook over low heat, stirring occasionally, until the peanut butter and marshmallows melt, about 5 minutes. Remove from the heat and fold in the cereal until fully coated.

3. Transfer the mixture to the prepared baking dish and lightly press it into an even layer. Place the jelly in a medium microwave-safe bowl and microwave on high for about 1 minute, stopping to stir halfway through, until soft and runny. Spoon the jelly over the cereal base, cover with plastic wrap, and refrigerate for 1 hour before slicing and serving.

CHAMPIONSHIP RINGS

Finally a dessert that's crafty without the stress of Pinterest-level abilities! It's as easy as laying out some pretzels, unwrapping chocolate kisses, keeping an eye on the oven (that part is super important but still easy), and pressing in some M&M's. A guaranteed score every time!

MAKES 48 RINGS

48 **circular** or **square pretzels**

48 **chocolate kisses**, any flavor

48 **milk chocolate M&M's**

1. Preheat the oven to 300°F with a rack in the center. Line a rimmed baking sheet with parchment paper or foil.

2. Place the pretzels on the prepared baking sheet in six rows of eight. Place a kiss in the center of each pretzel. Bake for 2 to 3 minutes, until the kisses are very soft but still holding their shape.

3. Remove the baking sheet from the oven and press an M&M into the center of each kiss. Chill in the refrigerator until the chocolate is set, about 5 minutes.

GRIDIRON CAKE

It's hard to say if this is dessert or art, but either way it's delicious. Ice the cake to make a football stadium, sprinkle green coconut to make a grassy field, and add candy players. You can have your cake and play on it, too.

SERVES 10 TO 12

Nonstick cooking spray

1 (15.25-ounce) box **cake mix**, plus additional ingredients according to box

2 cups **Buttercream Frosting**, homemade *(see page 150)* or store-bought

Food coloring

1 cup **sweetened coconut flakes**

1 (12-ounce) bag **white chocolate chips**

Chocolate candies, such as Hershey's Kisses and M&M's for decorating

1. Preheat the oven to 350°F with a rack in the center. Coat a rimmed baking sheet with nonstick spray. Line the bottom with parchment paper and spray again.

2. Mix the cake according to the package directions. Pour the batter into the prepared baking sheet and smooth the top. Bake according to the package instructions, until a toothpick inserted in the center comes out clean. Cool completely in the baking dish, about 2 hours.

3. Turn the cake out onto a rack. Peel off the parchment, then lay the pan on top and flip the cake back into the pan. Use a ruler to measure out a 4½-inch-long end zone at both ends of the cake. Use a paring knife to cut a shallow reference line for each end zone. The center field should be 9 inches in length.

4. Divide the frosting among four small bowls. Mix the frosting in three of the bowls with 2 to 4 drops of food coloring to create the green grass, your home team's colors, and the away team's colors. Leave the fourth bowl white. Place the coconut in a medium bowl, then add 4 drops of green food coloring and stir until evenly coated.

5. Use an offset spatula to spread the green frosting in the center between the end zones, and sprinkle the coconut grass evenly on top. Spread the team color frostings on the end zones (one on each side). Add the white frosting to a piping bag fitted with a plain tip and pipe white borders around the two end zones. (A zip-top pack with a small snip off the corner works, too!) Pipe a line across the middle of the cake, then equally divide the green with two more lines on each side.

6. To make the goal posts, line a baking sheet with parchment paper. Microwave ½ cup of the white chocolate chips in a small bowl for about 90 seconds, stopping to stir every 30 seconds. Carefully spoon the melted chocolate onto parchment paper, making 2 large U shapes attached to 2 thicker vertical bases. Chill in the refrigerator for 5 to 10 minutes, until set.

7. Place the remaining white chocolate chips on top of all the white lines. Use the chocolate candies to label the "HOME" and "AWAY" end zones and arrange the players on the field. Chill the cake until game time. Insert the goal posts at both end zones before serving.

Creamsicle

Key Lime Pie

Cinnamon Roll

Coconut Cake

SHOTGUN

SHOTGUN

Remember the song about a spoonful of sugar? A dessert shot helping the alcohol go down is basically the same principle. Based on four desserts as delicious as a warm cinnamon roll, tart key lime pie, sweet Creamsicle, and tropical coconut cake, these might go down a little too easy. You've been warned! Serve a crowd by multiplying and pre-batching the ingredients in a large jar. When it's time to serve, measure out 3 ounces for each pair of shots, then shake and serve.

=== EACH MAKES 2 SHOTS ===

Cinnamon Roll

1½ ounces **cinnamon whiskey**

1½ ounces **cream soda**

GO BIG: *Rim the shot glasses with vanilla icing, then dip in cinnamon sugar.*

Rim the glasses, if desired. Combine the cinnamon whiskey and cream soda in a cocktail shaker with ice. Shake until the outside of the shaker is frosted, then strain into the glasses and serve immediately.

Creamsicle

1 ounce **vanilla** or **whipped cream vodka**

1 ounce **orange soda**

1 ounce **lemon-lime soda**

GO BIG: *Rim the shot glasses with vanilla icing, then sprinkle with orange zest.*

Rim the glasses, if desired. Combine the vodka, orange soda, and lemon-lime soda in a cocktail shaker with ice. Shake until the outside of the shaker is frosted, then strain into the glasses and serve immediately.

Key Lime Pie

1 ounce **tequila**

1 ounce **vanilla** or **whipped cream vodka**

1 ounce **margarita mix**

GO BIG: *Rim the shot glasses with a lime, then dip in crushed graham crackers.*

Rim the glasses, if desired. Combine the tequila, vodka, and margarita mix in a cocktail shaker with ice. Shake until the outside of the shaker is frosted, then strain into the glasses and serve immediately.

Coconut Cake

1½ ounces **coconut rum**

1½ ounces **lemon-lime soda**

Splash of **grenadine**

GO BIG: *Rim the shot glasses with a lime, then dip in sweetened coconut flakes.*

Rim the glasses, if desired. Combine the rum, soda, and grenadine in a cocktail shaker with ice. Shake until the outside of the shaker is frosted, then strain into the glasses and serve immediately.

DRAFT PICKS

There are times when you can't decide between a beer or a cocktail. To that we ask, "Why not both?!" These are beer-inspired takes on favorite cocktails like Bee's Knees, mimosas, and margaritas—a day drink to please everyone's tastes! And we wouldn't forget a perfectly refreshing shandy for the days when you're taking it easy. Ice in beer is usually a party foul, but ice in a beer cocktail is a different story. Go ahead and load up that glass!

EACH MAKES 1 DRINK

Beer's Knees

1½ ounces **gin**

Juice of 1 **lemon**

1 tablespoon **honey**

1 (12-ounce) bottle **light beer**, such as Heineken

GO BIG: *Rim the glass with honey and garnish with an orange round.*

Combine the gin, lemon juice, and honey in a pint glass and stir until the honey is dissolved. Fill the cup with ice and top off with beer. Stir again and serve.

Bromosas

¼ cup **orange juice**

1 (12-ounce) bottle **American lager beer**, such as Miller High Life

GO BIG: *Rim the glass with an orange, then dip it in Tang for an extra boost of color and flavor.*

Fill a pint glass with ice. Add the orange juice and top off with the beer. Stir and serve.

Beergaritas

1½ ounces **tequila**

1 ounce **Cointreau**

Juice of 1 **lime**

1 (12-ounce) bottle **Mexican lager beer**, such as Corona

GO BIG: *Freeze margarita mix in ice cube trays and add them for an extra kick.*

Combine the tequila, Cointreau, and lime juice in a pint glass and stir to combine. Add ice and top off with beer. Stir and serve.

Ginger Shandy

1 (12-ounce) bottle **ginger beer**

1 (12-ounce) bottle **Belgian-style witbier**, such as Hoegaarden

GO BIG: *Rim the glass with a lime wedge, then dip it in a mixture of freshly grated ginger and turbinado sugar.*

Fill a pint glass with ice. Add half of the ginger beer and top off with half of the beer. Stir and serve. Keep the bottles handy to refill as needed.

Bromosas

Beer's Knees

Beergaritas

Ginger Shandy

DRAFT PICKS

HAIL MARY

When you're still feeling the night before on the day of, there's nothing like a Bloody Mary to kick the life back into you. We start with the formula for a Perfect Bloody, then flip the script with buffalo-, Caesar-, and michelada-inspired cocktails to keep things spicy. If homemade bloody mix isn't in the cards, just stir together a 750 ml bottle of vodka with 72 ounces of store-bought Bloody Mary mix. (But you already know homemade is far superior.)

The Perfect Bloody

1 recipe **Perfect Bloody Mix** *(recipe follows)*

Pepperoncini, for serving

Blue cheese–stuffed olives, for serving

Lemon wedges, for serving

GO BIG: *Rim the glass with a lemon wedge and dip half the rim in celery salt and half in smoked paprika.*

For each serving, fill a pint glass with ice, then add 8 ounces of bloody mix. Stir and garnish with pepperoncini, olives, and lemons to serve.

Buffalo Mary

½ cup **buffalo wing sauce** (we like Frank's RedHot)

1 recipe **Perfect Bloody Mix** *(recipe follows)*

Celery stalks, for serving

Carrot sticks, for serving

GO BIG: *A couple buffalo wings for garnish? There's no rule that says you can't!*

Stir the wing sauce into the bloody mix. For each serving, fill a pint glass with ice, then add 8 ounces of bloody mix. Stir and garnish with celery and carrots to serve.

Bloody Caesar

1 recipe **Perfect Bloody Mix** *(recipe follows)*

Romaine hearts, for serving

Cooked bacon, for serving

Lemon wedges, for serving

GO BIG: *Rim the glass with a lemon wedge, then dip the rim in a mixture of black pepper and grated Parmesan cheese.*

For each serving, fill a pint glass with ice, then add 8 ounces of bloody mix. Stir and garnish with romaine, bacon, and lemons to serve.

Marychelada

Tajín

Lime wedges

1 recipe **Perfect Bloody Mix** *(recipe follows)*

6 (12-ounce) cans **Mexican lager beer**

GO BIG: *Add a mini Coronita upside down in the glass to keep the beer flowing with every sip.*

Add the Tajín to a small plate, then rim the glasses with lime wedges and dip them in the Tajín. For each serving, fill a pint glass with ice, add 8 ounces of bloody mix, and top off with half a beer. Stir and serve.

Perfect Bloody Mix

MAKES 103 OUNCES

1 (64-ounce) bottle **tomato juice**

½ cup **prepared horseradish**

½ cup **Worcestershire sauce**

½ cup **fresh lemon juice**

2 tablespoons **freshly ground black pepper**

2 tablespoons **smoked paprika**

1 teaspoon **cayenne pepper**

1 (750 ml) bottle **vodka**

In a large jar or pitcher, combine the tomato juice, horseradish, Worcestershire sauce, lemon juice, black pepper, paprika, and cayenne, and stir well. Add the vodka and stir again. Cover and store in the fridge until ready to serve. Give everything a good mix before using.

TOUCHDOWN TIP: *To go all the way here, substitute Clamato juice for tomato juice in your Bloody mix.*

Marychelada

Buffalo Mary

The Perfect
Bloody

Bloody Caesar

HAIL MARY

Swiss Don't Miss

Hottie Toddy

Luck of the Irish

Flannel shirt

WE ARE HAPPY TO SERVE YOU

HUDDLE UP

HUDDLE UP

Only a chilly day, a hot drink is the real MVP. Boozy apple cider, Irish coffee, spiked hot chocolate, and hot toddies come in handy when you're warming up for the big game.

Flannel Shirt

1 gallon **apple cider**

4½ cups **caramel vodka** or **spiced rum**

1 cup (packed) **light brown sugar**

2 tablespoons **apple pie spice**

GO BIG: *Drizzle each mug with caramel and garnish with an apple cider donut.*

Combine the cider, vodka, brown sugar, and pie spice in a slow cooker and stir until the sugar has dissolved. Cover and set to warm. Let warm for at least 1 hour before serving.

Luck of the Irish

1 cup **instant coffee**

1 cup packed **light brown sugar**

4½ cups **Irish whiskey**

GO BIG: *Top each mug with a dollop of whipped cream and a dusting of cocoa powder.*

Combine the instant coffee, brown sugar, whiskey, and 1 gallon water in a slow cooker. Stir until the coffee and sugar have dissolved. Cover and set to warm. Let warm for at least 1 hour before serving.

Swiss Don't Miss

24 packets (or 4 cups) **hot chocolate mix**

4½ cups **marshmallow vodka** or **whipped cream vodka**

GO BIG: *Add a handful of mini marshmallows and a candy cane stirrer to each mug.*

Combine the hot chocolate mix, vodka, and 1 gallon water in a slow cooker and stir until the hot chocolate mix has dissolved. Cover and set to warm. Let warm for at least 1 hour before serving.

Hottie Toddy

1½ cups **honey**

4½ cups **rum** or **whiskey**

16 to 20 **ginger tea bags**

GO BIG: *Add a lemon round, cinnamon stick, and star anise pod to each mug.*

Combine the honey, rum, and 1 gallon water in a slow cooker and stir until the honey has dissolved. Add the tea bags, cover, and set to warm. Let warm for at least 1 hour and remove the tea bags before serving.

TOUCHDOWN TIP: *Use a portable slow cooker to keep these toasty warm. These recipes are made for a 6-quart vessel (or larger).*

DROP KICK

There's something about a bomb shot that makes the whole operation run smoother. Maybe it's the chaser, but we like to think it's the excitement of game time. These delicious shots will get you pumped up and ready to go. Hut-hut-hike!

Skittle Bomb

1½ ounces **Cointreau**

4 ounces **Red Bull** (about ½ can)

GO BIG: *If you're preparing a line of shots, add a different drop of food coloring to each glass to create a rainbow effect.*

Add the Cointreau to a shot glass. Drop the shot into a glass filled with Red Bull.

Darth Jäger

1½ ounces **Jägermeister**

½ cup **sparkling apple cider**

GO BIG: *Swap the apple cider with bright red fruit punch for a lightsaber effect.*

Add the Jägermeister to a shot glass. Place a rocks glass over the shot, then invert the glass so the shot is suspended before filling with the apple cider.

Dew Drop

1½ ounces **Midori**

4 ounces **Mountain Dew** (about ⅓ can)

GO BIG: *Pair it with a tequila shot chased with the Dew Drop for an extra kick.*

Add the Midori to a shot glass. Drop the shot into a glass filled with Mountain Dew.

Glitter Bomb

1½ ounces **Goldschläger**

4 ounces **Red Bull** (about ½ can)

GO BIG: *Up the sparkle factor with edible luster dust.*

Add the Goldschläger to a shot glass. Drop the shot into a glass filled with Red Bull.

Skittle Bomb

Dew Drop

Bull

110

DROP KICK

INDEX

ACKNOWLEDGMENTS

Teamwork makes the dream work, and this book is a testament to that motto.
Three cheers for an All-Star lineup!

Writer and Original Recipe Developer

Casey Elsass

Styling and Photography

Lauren Volo

Monica Pierini

Maeve Sheridan

Christina Zhang

Emma Rowe

Aliyah Pair

Tsering Dolma

Union Square & Co.

Amanda Englander

Raphael Geroni

Melissa Farris

Scott Amerman

Terence Campo

Caroline Hughes